T0079837

HUMMUS

Edible

Series Editor: Andrew F. Smith

EDIBLE is a revolutionary series of books dedicated to food and drink that explores the rich history of cuisine. Each book reveals the global history and culture of one type of food or beverage.

Already published

Apple Erika Janik, *Avocado* Jeff Miller, *Banana* Lorna Piatti-Farnell, *Barbecue* Jonathan Deutsch and Megan J. Elias, *Beans* Nathalie Rachel Morris, *Beef* Lorna Piatti-Farnell, *Beer* Gavin D. Smith, *Berries* Heather Arndt Anderson, *Biscuits and Cookies* Anastasia Edwards, *Brandy* Becky Sue Epstein, *Bread* William Rubel, *Cabbage* Meg Muckenhoupt, *Cake* Nicola Humble, *Caviar* Nichola Fletcher, *Champagne* Becky Sue Epstein, *Cheese* Andrew Dalby, *Chillies* Heather Arndt Anderson, *Chocolate* Sarah Moss and Alexander Badenoch, *Cocktails* Joseph M. Carlin, *Coffee* Jonathan Morris, *Corn* Michael Owen Jones, *Curry* Colleen Taylor Sen, *Dates* Nawal Nasrallah, *Doughnut* Heather Delancey Hunwick, *Dumplings* Barbara Gallani, *Edible Flowers* Constance L. Kirker and Mary Newman, *Edible Insects* Gina Louise Hunter, *Eggs* Diane Toops, *Fats* Michelle Phillipov, *Figs* David C. Sutton, *Foie Gras* Norman Kolpas, *Game* Paula Young Lee, *Gin* Lesley Jacobs Solmonson, *Hamburger* Andrew F. Smith, *Herbs* Gary Allen, *Herring* Kathy Hunt, *Honey* Lucy M. Long, *Hot Dog* Bruce Kraig, *Hummus* Harriet Nussbaum, *Ice Cream* Laura B. Weiss, *Jam, Jelly and Marmalade* Sarah B. Hood, *Lamb* Brian Yarvin, *Lemon* Toby Sonneman, *Lobster* Elisabeth Townsend, *Melon* Sylvia Lovegren, *Milk* Hannah Velten, *Moonshine* Kevin R. Kosar, *Mushroom* Cynthia D. Bertelsen, *Mustard* Demet Güzey, *Nuts* Ken Albala, *Offal* Nina Edwards, *Olive* Fabrizia Lanza, *Onions and Garlic* Martha Jay, *Oranges* Clarissa Hyman, *Oyster* Carolyn Tillie, *Pancake* Ken Albala, *Pasta and Noodles* Kantha Shelke, *Pickles* Jan Davison, *Pie* Janet Clarkson, *Pineapple* Kaori O'Connor, *Pizza* Carol Helstosky, *Pomegranate* Damien Stone, *Pork* Katharine M. Rogers, *Potato* Andrew F. Smith, *Pudding* Jeri Quinzio, *Rice* Renee Marton, *Rum* Richard Foss, *Saffron* Ramin Ganeshram, *Salad* Judith Weinraub, *Salmon* Nicolaas Mink, *Sandwich* Bee Wilson, *Sauces* Maryann Tebben, *Sausage* Gary Allen, *Seaweed* Kaori O'Connor, *Shrimp* Yvette Florio Lane, *Soda and Fizzy Drinks* Judith Levin, *Soup* Janet Clarkson, *Spices* Fred Czarra, *Sugar* Andrew F. Smith, *Sweets and Candy* Laura Mason, *Tea* Helen Saberi, *Tequila* Ian Williams, *Tomato* Clarissa Hyman, *Truffle* Zachary Nowak, *Vanilla* Rosa Abreu-Runkel, *Vodka* Patricia Herlihy, *Water* Ian Miller, *Whiskey* Kevin R. Kosar, *Wine* Marc Millon, *Yoghurt* June Hersh

Hummus

A Global History

Harriet Nussbaum

REAKTION BOOKS

For my parents, Ralph and Rosemary, and in memory of my grandmother Nora, who also enjoyed experimenting in the kitchen

Published by Reaktion Books Ltd
Unit 32, Waterside
44–48 Wharf Road
London N1 7UX, UK
www.reaktionbooks.co.uk

Printed and bound in India by Replika Press Pvt. Ltd

A catalogue record for this book is available from the British Library

ISBN 978 1 78914 462 8

Contents

Introduction

I don't remember the first time I tasted hummus myself. As a child growing up in the 1990s – and primarily in the UK – I belong to the first generation in Europe for whom hummus was an ordinary, everyday childhood food. The first pots of hummus even appeared in UK supermarkets the year I was born. I have many early memories of eating meze in Lebanese and Turkish restaurants: it was the kind of food that my parents liked to eat. They had both briefly studied in the Middle East, and had retained a fondness for the dishes they had enjoyed there, which they later shared with their children. My mother and my paternal grandmother both had well-thumbed copies of Claudia Roden's *A Book of Middle Eastern Food* on their shelves and we always had a jar of tahini in the cupboard.

Years later, at school, hummus was an occasional and much-welcomed treat: my friends and I would eagerly anticipate the gourmet delights of Wednesday Salad Bar. Week in, week out, this salad selection boasted (among other things) a jumble of avocado, rocket and chopped strawberries, new potatoes with butter and herbs, bowls of raisins and toasted seeds for sweet and crunchy salad toppings, and a large tub of hummus. Looking back, this hummus was fridge-cold and inexcusably grainy, but we embraced it heartily – for the most part because it was not the tuna mayonnaise or grated cheddar that we were met with on other days of the week. Hummus was just exotic enough to be a lunchtime treat, while being sufficiently familiar to be popular with a queue of hungry teenagers.

But it was not until I began to travel to the Middle East in my early twenties that I really refined my hummus palate. While studying Arabic and Hebrew at university, I moved to Egypt for a year of language immersion. Though hummus can be found all over Cairo, Egyptians are equally fond of their chickpeas as part of a dish called *koshari* – a carbohydrate-heavy mixture in which the legumes are combined with rice, pasta and lentils, and accompanied with crispy fried onions and a spicy sauce. The best hummus I found in Egypt was served at a Lebanese restaurant in an area of Cairo known as Garden City: a smooth and well-flavoured dish accompanied by soft, freshly baked flatbreads, hot from the oven. That hummus set the bar for all the hummuses to come. In the months and years that followed my studies in Egypt, I travelled through the Levant and the eastern Mediterranean, tasting that creamy chickpea favourite in every place I visited.

After finishing my degree I moved from Oxford to London, where I quickly discovered the culinary pleasures of Edgware Road: a little slice of the Middle East, with all its familiar smells and flavours. Of course, hummus was all around me in London – in sandwich wraps at cafés, on sharing platters in pubs, at picnic parties and stacked high in plastic tubs in every supermarket. And while the hummus I ate in Levantine restaurants was almost invariably served in the same way – scraped around the edge of a small red clay bowl, garnished with olive oil, paprika and parsley, and served with flatbreads and pickled vegetables – supermarket hummus was mostly used as a dip, eaten straight out of the pot with

Tub of industrially made supermarket hummus, a popular dip and snack food.

anything from carrots to crisps. The traditional Levantine hummus consisted of just four main ingredients (chickpeas, tahini, lemon and garlic), but pre-packaged hummus could be flavoured with anything from peas to peri-peri.

My love for hummus and hummus culture was reinforced on meeting my Israeli partner. One of the first compliments he ever paid to me was that I scooped hummus with a piece of pitta like a professional. Together from our home in Berlin we would go out to eat a dish of hummus or *musabbaha* (warm hummus with whole chickpeas) at a small Arab restaurant, ordering a toasted flatbread with olive oil and *za'atar* on the side. Alternatively, we would make fresh hummus at home using Lebanese tahini from one of the many Arab food shops in our neighbourhood and chickpeas we had soaked overnight. And although hummus was available to me in the supermarkets of Berlin as it had been in London, I stopped buying it altogether because it simply couldn't compare to

Traditional Levantine restaurant in Berlin, where hummus is eaten alongside other meze dishes.

the real thing. What's more, I had already learnt to appreciate that fundamental Levantine ritual: going out to eat hummus. The simple pleasure of going out to eat a plate of freshly made hummus is somewhat comparable to a summer afternoon stroll to savour an ice cream. It is not merely a question of quality (though quality is important) but of absorbing the atmosphere and environment that go hand in hand with the food or dish in question. Most ice cream, no matter how delicious, will not taste as good if eaten from a frozen tub at home.

These days, with two small children to cook for, I am the first to admit to opening jars or tins of chickpeas when I need to make hummus quickly. But when I can (and remember to), I take great pleasure in soaking a large container of dried chickpeas in water last thing at night, before I go to bed. Like preparing a bowl of bircher muesli for the following morning, or putting a sourdough loaf into the fridge to proof

Bowl of dried chickpeas soaking in water before cooking.

overnight, it is slow food at its very best. In a world in which we often throw dinner together in fifteen minutes, there is something very enjoyable about a meal that needs a day's notice.

Hummus is a wonderful dish in so many ways: it's nutritious, filling, versatile, inexpensive and sustainable. With the help of a decent blender or food processor it is also extremely easy to prepare, and requires little accompaniment to constitute a wholesome meal. If desired, however, there are endless variations on these accompaniments: virtually every grain and vegetable will work with hummus. To continue to call it a dip is simply an injustice. Hummus is a great source of plant-based protein, carbohydrates, healthy fats and abundant minerals. It is a staple for our times, and, luckily for us, it just so happens that it also tastes delicious.

If you have only ever tried hummus from a supermarket tub, I first urge you to taste it freshly made in the traditional Levantine style. Then, if the mood strikes you, try making your own hummus at home. Next, engage your nearest and dearest in lengthy conversations about the various characteristics of your favourite hummus – taste, texture, temperature, toppings – because the next best thing to eating hummus is talking about it.

I

When Chickpeas Met Tahini

The word 'hummus' (sometimes spelled 'houmous' or 'hommos' in English) comes from the Arabic term *ḥummuṣ*, literally meaning 'chickpeas'. Though we have no historical evidence of the preparation of any kind of chickpea-based dip or paste until the medieval period, we can be sure that chickpeas were widely cultivated and eaten in different forms in the Near and Middle East from ancient times. The cultivated chickpea is an edible seed from a small flowering plant known botanically as *Cicer arietinum*. This plant has two types: desi and kabuli. Desi, native to South and East Asia, has small, dark seeds, while kabuli has larger seeds that are lighter in colour and is native to West Asia (including the Mediterranean region). Both types are annual plants, yielding one crop of chickpeas per year. Along with soya beans, peanuts and alfalfa, chickpeas belong to the family of legume plants known as Fabaceae or Leguminosae.

According to archaeological findings, the wild chickpea may first have been domesticated as a crop some 7,000 years ago in the northeastern Mediterranean region (modern-day Syria and Turkey). This early domestication almost certainly had a profound impact on the population growth in the area. Chickpeas became a simple, affordable, high-protein staple that could be eaten in combination with locally cultivated

The Mediterranean basin: hummus is native to the cuisines of the eastern Mediterranean region.

grains, such as wheat and barley. From the Near East, the chickpea spread as a cultivated crop to other areas, such as the Middle East, South Asia and North Africa. By the Bronze Age (from the fourth to second millennium BCE), chickpeas were grown across the region, from Greece in the west to India in the east. Chickpea cultivation was later introduced to Italy, France, Spain and other parts of mainland Europe.

Chickpeas were a popular food in ancient Egypt, classical Greece and in the Roman Empire, where they were affordable, widely consumed and prepared in a number of different ways. Most simply, they could be consumed raw, salted or roasted. In ancient times chickpeas were often eaten after the evening meal, and their nutritional benefits were lauded by

Chickpeas, the principal ingredient in hummus.

Constantino Sabbati, 'Chickpea (*Cicer sativum / arietinum*)', hand-coloured engraving from Giorgio Bonelli and Niccoló Martelli, *Hortus Romanus . . .*, vol. VII (1793).

the Greek philosophers Plato and Socrates. Roman writers and physicians likewise remarked on the numerous benefits of consuming chickpeas. Galen, writing in the second century CE, asserts that chickpeas were extremely nutritious (more so than beans), even claiming that their consumption could cause an increase in sperm production.[1] He specifically mentions that chickpeas were consumed both dried and ground into flour, and cooked in a soup. The legume continued to be widely eaten in southern Europe through late antiquity and into the medieval period: from there it was brought to the Americas by the Spanish and Portuguese in the sixteenth century. Today chickpeas are eaten across the world, with India, Australia, the United States and Turkey leading production. A humble but highly nutritious legume, the chickpea forms an integral part of many different cuisines worldwide.

Miniature from a 14th-century Greek manuscript depicting the banquet at the marriage of Alexander the Great and Roxane.

Peasant picking chickpeas, from a 14th-century edition of the medieval health handbook *Tacuinum sanitatis*.

The full Arabic name for the popular dish made from crushed chickpeas is *ḥummuṣ bi-ṭaḥina*, or 'chickpeas with tahini', since these are the two primary ingredients of the dish. Tahini is an oily paste made from ground sesame seeds that is used to flavour many dishes, salads and sauces in Middle Eastern cuisine. Its name is derived from the Arabic verb *ṭaḥ ana* – 'to grind' – and it is known to much of the world as tahini (rather than tahina) on the basis of the Levantine Arabic pronunciation of the final vowel (and via the Greek language, which employs the same term). Sesame seeds and sesame oil have long been used across the Levantine region and beyond, and archaeological and literary evidence of this practice has been found from ancient India, Egypt and the Near East, as well as from classical Greece and the Roman Empire. While we cannot be sure exactly when and where sesame seeds were first ground to a paste, we know that tahini was a popular ingredient in Levantine cuisine from at least the tenth century CE.

In its simplest form, the only additional ingredients required for hummus are garlic, lemon juice, a pinch of salt and a final drizzle of olive oil. Garlic has been used in Near and Middle Eastern cooking for thousands of years. One of the earliest recipes calling for its use is preserved on a Babylonian clay tablet dating from around 1750 BCE. This recipe requires pounded garlic in the preparation of a meat pie. Garlic was also popular with the ancient Egyptians, Greeks and Romans, who gave it to their slaves, athletes and soldiers in order to increase their strength.

Lemons, however, arrived on the Levantine culinary stage a little later. The first literary reference to a lemon comes from an Arabic document written in the tenth century CE, which describes the lemon tree as being sensitive to cold. The fruit is likely to have originated in India, along with citrons and some kinds of bitter orange. From India, citrus fruits may have first travelled westwards by sea, leaving the Indus Valley and arriving in Mesopotamia. Lemons were only widely cultivated in the Mediterranean after the spread of the Islamic Empire into that region (from the seventh century CE).

Sesame seeds are ground to make tahini, an essential element of hummus.

Different varieties of tahini in a Middle Eastern food shop.

Olive oil – used to garnish hummus – is one of the most well-established Mediterranean staples, joining bread and wine to form the so-called Mediterranean triad (based on the widespread local crops of olives, wheat and grapes). Like chickpeas, olives have been part of Levantine food culture from its very beginnings. As we shall see, despite the fact that all the key hummus ingredients have been available in the region from the tenth century CE at the very latest, there is no indication that they were used together to make hummus as we know it today until much later.

Regardless of this evidence, some have attempted to claim that hummus has far more ancient origins. In 2007 the Israeli author Meir Shalev published an article in Hebrew entitled '*Ha-hummus hu shelanu*' ('Hummus Is Ours'), arguing for the existence of hummus in the biblical period. According to Shalev, the Book of Ruth contains a reference to hummus. In one story, the biblical figure Boaz invites Ruth to dip her

Illumination by Taddeo Crivelli showing Ruth and Boaz in the field, from the Bible of Borso d'Este, *c.* 1455–61.

morsel of bread into *ḥomeṣ* – a word that the New Revised Standard Version of the Bible gives as 'sour wine' and that has the meaning 'vinegar' in modern Hebrew. Shalev proposes that they are, rather, dipping their bread into an ancient form of hummus.

Dependent on context, modern Hebrew speakers use the word *ḥummuṣ* to mean chickpeas or hummus. But this term has been relatively recently borrowed from Arabic: an alternative word, *ḥimṣa*, was once used in Hebrew with the meaning 'chickpeas'. Shalev claims that the words *ḥummuṣ*, *ḥimṣa* and *ḥomeṣ* are all based on the same Semitic three-letter root, *ḥ-m-ṣ*, further leading to his assertion that Boaz and Ruth were dipping their bread in hummus rather than vinegar. He connects the meanings by remarking that chickpeas sour quickly (and therefore taste similar to vinegar and other such foods), proposing that they gained their Hebrew name this way.

Despite the connection between these words, there is no reason to assume that *ḥomeṣ* – which ordinarily implies wine vinegar – has anything to do with hummus in the Book of Ruth. First, while it might not have the literal meaning of pure vinegar in the context (bread dipped in vinegar does not sound especially appetizing), it may well suggest a dish seasoned or preserved with vinegar or indeed any other sour or fermented food. Furthermore, even if *ḥomeṣ* does have the meaning of 'chickpeas' in the Book of Ruth, as they were surely eaten in biblical times, there is no reason to suggest that these chickpeas would have been prepared in a manner similar to hummus. Certainly Ruth and Boaz were not dipping a pitta into a smooth and creamy mixture of ground chick-peas, tahini, lemon and garlic and rounding the meal off with a plate of freshly fried falafel. Shalev's attempt to connect modern-day hummus with the world of ancient Israel belongs firmly to the twenty-first-century debate over the ownership of hummus (but more on that story later).

The simple practice of mixing chickpeas with tahini may originally have evolved as a method of substituting pulses for meat. During Lent, many denominations of Christians in the Levantine region abstain from all animal products – theirs is the original vegan Middle Eastern menu. The writer and food historian Charles Perry has suggested that the combination of chickpeas and tahini may have first been used by Christian communities during the Lenten fast.[2]

As he notes, tahini was a popular ingredient from around the tenth century onwards, and was often used in flavouring meat and poultry dishes. Christians might have added it to their Lenten bowl of chickpeas, as they ordinarily did to their meat, though such a dish could have been served and eaten quite differently from hummus. As a replacement for meat, the chickpeas might just as easily have been eaten whole, with the tahini providing a sauce. In such a case, mashing the chickpeas and combining them with tahini and other ingredients would have been a secondary step on the path to making hummus.

According to the medieval Arabic recipes given below, in the thirteenth and fourteenth centuries (if not before) there was a fashion for elaborate and highly flavoured dishes containing an abundance of herbs, spices and nuts. In this sense, though medieval mashed-chickpea dishes bear a resemblance to hummus, they look and taste quite different. Eventually, as culinary fashions changed, the combination of puréed chickpeas and tahini became a far simpler affair, requiring only a couple of additional ingredients.

The earliest literary references to a medieval chickpea and tahini dish come from two Arabic cookbooks dating from the thirteenth and fourteenth centuries respectively. Arabic literature boasts a particular wealth of medieval cookbooks, with

Spices were a popular addition to medieval Arab courtly cuisine.

the earliest surviving work dating from the tenth century. These recipe collections were compiled primarily to record fashionable and popular dishes of the time. The custom of writing down recipes is thought to have been adopted from Persian aristocratic culture, which was highly influential on the courtly culture of the Abbasid Caliphs of Baghdad, who reigned from 750 to 1258 CE. Persia was conquered by the Muslim armies in the seventh century, putting an end to the Sassanid Empire and to the prevalence of the Zoroastrian religion. Persian, however, survived as the dominant language – indeed, of the vast number of territories that were conquered during the first century of Islam, it was the only one that did not adopt Arabic. The elegant and sophisticated cuisine of the medieval Islamic world drew much inspiration from the food of Persia, incorporating popular Persian ingredients and flavour combinations. Furthermore, the medieval Islamic Empire was vast, and also incorporated the Iberian peninsula, North Africa, a number of Mediterranean islands, the Arabian Peninsula, Syria and Mesopotamia. This opened up endless opportunities for cultural exchange – not only in the trading of ingredients but in the movement of peoples, and with them culinary practices and regional recipes.

Alongside the composition of Arabic cookbooks in the Abbasid period, several other literary forms explored the subject of food, including poetry: traditionally the most respected and sophisticated form of Arabic literature. In addition to this, medieval Arab writers were also responsible for a great number of medical books concerned with the effects of various foods on the body. Collectively these works indicate that during the Abbasid period there was a strong interest in food, eating and culinary culture that was unparalleled elsewhere in the world at this time.

One Arabic medical book composed in Baghdad in 1224 describes a medicine to cure weakness made from honey and water and a digestive remedy made of pressed grapes, brine and an onion-like herb.

The courtly cuisine recorded in early Arabic cookbooks has been neatly characterized by the food historian Claudia Roden in her introduction to *The New Book of Middle Eastern Food* (1985). Roden notes that the courtly cuisine of the Abbasid period used particularly expensive ingredients which were eaten almost exclusively by the elite, including rice and sugar. What's more, even where simple, everyday ingredients like chickpeas and other pulses were used, the dish was made rich and elaborate with the addition of luxury foodstuffs such as nuts, spices or meat. Furthermore, the techniques used in preparing these dishes were also sophisticated, from preserving foods in one manner to crystallizing them in another. In the case of early hummus recipes, the chickpeas are crushed or ground to a smooth paste, presenting a more elaborate and technically professional way of serving a simple ingredient.

The presentation of medieval courtly dishes was also important, and guidelines were given for the proper and correct way of serving a particular dish. As regards recipes for an early form of hummus, in some instances the dish is topped with a number of different garnishes in addition to the traditional seasoning of olive oil. Recipes from courtly cuisine in this period may be broadly characterized as being complex: the simple flavours favoured in haute cuisine today – achieved by allowing a few good-quality ingredients to shine – were simply not fashionable.

Two medieval Arabic cookbooks, from Syria and Egypt respectively, contain recipes for a dish known as *hummus kasa* (sometimes *kisa*), containing chickpeas and tahini in combination with various nuts and spices. The term *kasa* (or *kisa*) may be translated as 'garment' and this name may reflect the thick consistency of the dish – not so much a smooth dip as a solid chickpea paste flavoured with all manner of ingredients. While this naturally yields a dish that is quite different from *hummus bi-tahina*, it is nonetheless the first literary example we have of this combination of ingredients. Furthermore, in some instances the serving instructions indicate that this kind of dish was a precursor to hummus. As with many medieval Arab recipes, some elements of the dish bear particular resemblance to ones we can recognize in modern dishes, while others appear quite different.

The first recipe comes from the thirteenth-century *Kitāb al-Wuṣla ilā l-ḥabīb fī waṣf al-ṭayyibāt wa-l-ṭīb* (translated as *Book of the Relation with the Beloved in the Description of the Best Dishes and Spices*, although the Arabic title rhymes and is infinitely more catchy). This work is thought to have been written in Syria by a certain Ibn al-'Adim (1192–1262), placing its composition towards the end of the reign of the Ayyubid dynasty or the early years of the Mamluk one (both of these dynasties ruled in Egypt and the Levant). This cookbook makes reference to recipes of diverse origin, indicating that it was written in the context of a pluralistic society in which culinary cultures intermingled. The work has been translated to English by Charles Perry under the beautifully crafted title *Scents and Flavors the Banqueter Favors*. It gives a recipe for *hummus kisa* that includes crushed chickpeas in combination with tahini, vinegar, ground walnuts, lemon juice (as well as minced preserved lemons), fresh parsley and mint, olive oil and various spices – including coriander seed, caraway, cinnamon, pepper and ginger. The dish is garnished with pistachios, olive oil, parsley, cinnamon, rose hips and whole chickpeas, and should be thick enough that it can be sliced and eaten on bread.[3]

Of course, this recipe for *hummus kisa* contains many ingredients not found in *hummus bi-tahina* as it is eaten today. Like all the medieval recipes given here, it also contains no garlic, despite the fact that garlic had long been available in the region. Furthermore, the texture described is different from that of the hummus we know and eat today, being solid enough to be 'cut up' rather than scooped or spread. Nonetheless, many of the essential elements of hummus are there: crushed chickpeas, lemon, tahini and the essential garnish of olive oil and whole chickpeas.

Charles Perry has also been responsible for the translation of the fourteenth-century *Kitāb Waṣf al-Aṭ'ima al-Mu'tada* (The Description of Familiar Foods). This work gives a recipe for Egyptian *hummus kasa*. According to the manuscript preserved at the Topkapi Palace in Istanbul, it was completed on 30 November 1373 in Cairo. In its compilation of recipes this work drew on a number of different sources, absorbing and adapting recipes from earlier Arabic cookbooks. The recipe for *hummus kasa* is similar to that seen in the Syrian work above, describing a thick, solid paste of crushed chickpeas, tahini, vinegar, lemon, nuts, herbs and spices. In this instance, the recommendation is to roll the mixture out flat before leaving it overnight.[4] The recipe differs from the previous one in a few small details, including the addition of thyme, hazelnuts, almonds and olives, but the overall end-product is remarkably similar.

Rue, a herb which was used in medieval chickpea dishes.

Another thirteenth-century work, *Kanz al-Fawā'id fī tanwī' al-mawā'id* (The Treasure of Useful Advice for the Composition of a Varied Table), was compiled in Egypt under the rule of the Mamluks. It likewise contains a number of recipes from different geographical regions (alongside many local Egyptian dishes). This work gives a somewhat pared-down version of the dish of puréed chickpeas, omitting the tahini and nuts but retaining a great number of herbs and spices, as well as vinegar and preserved lemons. The only additional ingredient called for in this particular medieval chickpea dish is chopped rue, a herb widely used in the late antique and medieval periods for culinary and medicinal purposes.

This recipe, given as 'puree of chickpeas with cinnamon and ginger', appears in Lilia Zaouali's *Medieval Cuisine of the Islamic World*. The recipe suggests pushing the mashed chickpeas through a wheat sieve (if necessary) to produce a finer purée, and seasoning the final chickpea mixture with good-quality olive oil.[5] This medieval dish thus appears closer to modern-day hummus in its texture, consistency and manner of serving, although it lacks the crucial element of tahini. However, in the latter respect it does bear some resemblance to an alternative dish of puréed chickpeas eaten in Egypt and elsewhere, which combines chickpeas with lemon, garlic and cumin but no tahini. The author, Colette Rossant, describes this simpler version of hummus in her food memoir, *Apricots on the Nile* (2001), and Claudia Roden likewise mentioned it in her *Book of Middle Eastern Food* (1968). Like the recipes for *hummus kasa* given above, the medieval purée of chickpeas with cinnamon and ginger is highly flavoured, while the chickpea purée Rossant and Roden describe is extremely simple. Based on the evidence of the three medieval recipes, we can assume that elaborate and complex chickpea purée dishes were once popular and fashionable. Over time, complex

Illustration from an edition of Rashid-al-Din Hamadani's 14th-century historical work depicting the Mongols besieging Baghdad in 1258.

flavours gave way to simple ones, garlic became a favourite addition, and hummus as we know it was born.

Unfortunately for food historians, enthusiasm for Arabic culinary literature faded over the following centuries, as the so-called Islamic Golden Age came to an end. In 1258 Baghdad was sacked and conquered by Mongol armies, who destroyed the city's books and libraries. No real culture of cookbook writing re-emerged until the modern period, and there are limited literary sources from the centuries in between. Indeed, what literary sources we do possess often give us lists of produce and ingredients without describing the dishes they were used to prepare. The absence of relevant written materials means we cannot trace the development of hummus-like dishes continuously.

Although we cannot be sure of its exact origins, *hummus bi-tahina* as we know it today probably developed centuries

Egyptian wooden panel, 12th–15th century, used to record the sales of chickpeas, wheat and straw.

after the first recipe for *hummus kasa* was recorded, in the context of the Levantine region under Ottoman rule. Charles Perry has suggested that the traditional manner of serving hummus in the Levant – whipped up against the edges of a small red clay bowl – indicates that it was first produced for the ruling classes in an urban environment such as Beirut or (as Perry himself believes) Damascus.[6] As he has noted, eighteenth-century Damascus was a large city with a notable elite, for whom such a fine-dining dish might first have been intended.

The traditional clay hummus bowl allows the diner to eat the hummus conveniently using pieces of flatbread or other foods, but it also allows the chef to demonstrate that the hummus has been prepared to exactly the right consistency. If it were too stiff it would not coat the outside of the bowl smoothly, yet too liquid and it would drip down into the centre. In this sense, *hummus bi-tahina* does not resemble the folk dishes of the region (and especially of rural areas), but rather something more sophisticated and elegant.

Regardless of exactly where and when the first bowl of hummus was served, we can be sure that the combination

Frederic Leighton, *Old Damascus – Jews' Quarter*, also titled *Gathering Citrons*, 1873–4, oil on canvas.

Hummus is traditionally served whipped against the edges of a red clay bowl.

of the two primary ingredients had already been eaten for centuries. Sometime between the thirteenth and eighteenth centuries spices, herbs, nuts and vinegar gave way to garlic; and a light, creamy chickpea purée replaced the more solid pastes of the medieval period. Once hummus became popular it rapidly spread through the surrounding region, being adopted into the food cultures of the Levant and eventually the whole of the eastern Mediterranean region.

2

Hummus at Home

Hummus is native to the eastern end of the Mediterranean basin: from Egypt through Jordan, Israel, Palestine, Syria, Lebanon and, to a lesser extent, Turkey, Greece and Cyprus. The Syrian chef Mohammad Orfali believes the description of hummus as being 'Middle Eastern' fails to capture its true identity.[1] Orfali rather describes hummus as a food of the Levant: the area nestled between the Mediterranean sea, the Turkish Taurus mountains, Mesopotamia and the Arabian desert. Today the region corresponds to Syria, Lebanon, Palestine, Israel and Jordan. The problem with describing hummus as Middle Eastern is that it suggests the dish is native to a far broader region than is the case, often culturally (if not geographically) incorporating North Africa as well as the regions east and southeast of Syria. Hummus is not traditionally Omani or Moroccan, though you would certainly find it in urban restaurants and supermarkets in either country today. Furthermore, it isn't specifically Lebanese or Syrian either: it is a Levantine food that has been prepared and eaten across the region for centuries without belonging specifically to one place or another. National borders within the Levant are not necessarily indicative of distinct cuisines, having been relatively recently introduced (as a result of European colonization in the early twentieth century). The cuisines of the

Levantine region are closely overlapping and the food of urban regions in different countries may often have more in common than the food of urban and rural regions within the same country.

Though the Levant was undoubtedly home to the first dishes of *hummus bi-tahina*, close connections and cultural exchanges with the surrounding region meant that it rapidly spread to other parts of the Mediterranean and was adopted into local culinary repertoires. In the eighteenth century, when *hummus bi-tahina* is thought to have first been prepared, the whole of the eastern Mediterranean was united under Ottoman rule. It is not surprising that dishes which were popular in one Ottoman territory were adopted by others. Furthermore, generally speaking, the cuisines of the eastern Mediterranean boast many ingredients and flavours that stem from the same palate, using similar grains, pulses, fruits and vegetables. In this sense, hummus isn't out of place on a Greek table spread with stuffed vine leaves, taramasalata and tzatziki, and it is easy to see how it might have been smoothly incorporated into Greek meze.

Across the region hummus is traditionally prepared with the same four central ingredients (chickpeas, tahini, garlic and lemon), though the hummus itself may vary somewhat from place to place. Some favour a smoother texture, some prefer more lemon or garlic, others create a creamier dish by increasing the amount of tahini used. According to the author and food writer Anissa Helou, Syrian hummus does not traditionally contain garlic: only Syrian *hummus beiruti*, with the addition of chopped parsley, is a garlicky dish.[2] What's more, in some instances of hummus-making in the eastern Mediterranean, additional herbs or spices such as cumin may be added, and one Turkish variation even replaces the tahini with melted butter or yoghurt.

According to traditional preparation methods, the dried chickpeas must be soaked overnight, then drained and boiled in fresh water until they are soft. In many cases their papery skins are also removed before mixing – although this may seem a somewhat laborious task it is often carried out with the intention of achieving the smoothest hummus possible. The French-Syrian historian and researcher Farouk Mardam-Bey considers the removal or otherwise of the chickpea skins to be the most important question as far as hummus-making is concerned. In contrast, he deems the quantities of the key ingredients and the order of mixing to be relatively unimportant, stating: 'In the Middle East, everyone has their own

Chickpea skins are often removed in hummus-making in order to achieve a smoother purée.

Chickpeas, as the legume *Cicer arietinum*, grow in green pods, in which they may be roasted after harvesting.

hummus recipe. Our hummus recipe is no more authentic than any other.'[3] Anissa Helou likewise recommends removing the chickpea skins in pursuit of the creamiest hummus (although she admits to skipping this step herself). Helou suggests running cold water over the cooked chickpeas and lightly rubbing them to encourage the skins to float to the surface, from where they may be poured or skimmed off. 'Even if you manage to peel only half,' she comments, 'you will notice a difference.'[4] As far as the chickpeas are concerned, Helou does not cook hers from scratch, but rather uses jars of salted chickpeas without the addition of preservatives, which she finds to be equal in quality if a little more expensive.

Food writer and blogger Deb Perelman has an original solution for making smooth hummus without labouring over chickpea skins: chana dal. These dried split chickpeas, which can be purchased at Indian and other international food shops, are skin-free and only need to be soaked and cooked as other chickpeas would. As she notes: 'you can have the same effect as you get here from peeling chickpeas without that extra step. It's glorious.'[5]

With or without their skins, chickpeas form a central part of the Levantine diet, and as such are seen as a simple but essential staple. One Arabic proverb describing a wholly wasted effort states: 'He left the feast without even a chickpea.' And while hummus and falafel are well known to the rest of the world, countless other chickpea-based foods are popular within the region. Indeed, in their simplest form, chickpeas are eaten roasted and unadulterated in their green pods, having been grown and harvested locally. The Arab-Israeli chef Nof Atamna-Ismaeel remembers uprooting chickpea plants with her grandmother: the plants were bundled together and cooked over the embers of a fire, after which the

Roasted chickpeas can be added to savoury mixtures of nuts and seeds.

pods were removed and the warm, soft chickpeas could be eaten.[6] Roasted and salted chickpeas are added to mixed nuts, seeds and beans: savoury, moreish and perfect for snacking. Colourful roasted and sugar-coated chickpeas (often flavoured with rosewater) are a sweet treat popular in Lebanon, Palestine and Turkey, as well as Iran and Afghanistan.

As far as more substantial meals are concerned, *hummus balila*, a meze dish, is perhaps the simplest way of serving chickpeas – boiled until soft and then seasoned with lemon, garlic, cumin, olive oil and pine nuts. *Fattet hummus* is a popular Levantine dish based on small pieces of toasted or fried bread that are topped with warm chickpeas and yoghurt, often being seasoned with fresh mint and pine nuts. Combined with rice, onions, tomatoes and spices, chickpeas also make a popular filling for stuffed vegetables (known as *mahshi* in Arabic). A flavoursome mixture of rice, chickpeas, onions

Colourful sugar-coated chickpeas are a popular celebratory food in the Middle East.

Chickpeas are used in *fattet hummus*, a Levantine dish made with yoghurt and toasted bread.

and spices may also be combined with meat, and a similar dish retains the chickpeas and meat but substitutes burghul (cracked wheat) for rice. Chickpeas appear in snacks, soups, stews and salads – they are an indispensable ingredient in Levantine cuisine.

While all tahini is made from ground sesame seeds, it varies greatly in flavour and consistency. Tahini made from natural, unhulled sesame is much darker in colour, with the thick consistency of a nut butter and a very strong flavour. To thin this kind of tahini a great deal of water is required. Tahini made from hulled sesame, on the other hand, is lighter in colour, oilier and more liquid. This is the tahini that is generally favoured for the production of hummus. But for those who love hummus (and tahini), even within the broad sphere of hulled sesame tahini there are subtle but distinct differences from one brand to another, and most hummus-makers have a particular favourite. The quality and quantity of tahini used in making hummus have a significant effect on the overall flavour and texture of the end-product. Mohammad Orfali recalls how the freshly made hummus of his childhood in

Tahini may be made from sesame that is hulled or unhulled, which greatly affects the colour and flavour. Lighter varieties are preferred for making hummus.

Syria was available in two kinds: regular and excellent.[7] The excellent hummus contained a great deal more tahini.

Lemon juice and garlic, the other two key flavours of hummus, are widely used in Levantine cuisine. Lemon juice, olive oil and salt is a very popular dressing for all manner of salads, while preserved lemons feature in many cooked dishes. Garlic is used both raw and cooked and is a vital ingredients in soups, stews and sauces, and a number of other dishes. Lemon and garlic are used to season other chickpea-based dishes, but also as flavourings for tahini and tahini-based salads and sauces (in combination with aubergines or yoghurt, for example).

Regardless of the exact recipe, hummus in the eastern Mediterranean is eaten at room temperature (occasionally warm), and scooped up from the bowl with freshly baked bread. Though pitta is commonly assumed to be the traditional counterpart to hummus, eastern Mediterranean breads vary in size, shape, taste and texture. In Turkey a thicker, fluffier bread is favoured, while in Egypt the local *aish baladi* is made with both plain and wholemeal flours, giving a coarser-textured, slightly chewy flatbread. In Israel, slices of raw white onion are invariably served alongside warm pitta – both to be dipped into generous bowls of creamy hummus. As part of the meze eaten at the beginning of a meal, the Lebanese and Syrians often offer a large plate of raw and pickled vegetables such as lettuce, pepper, tomato and radish. These crunchy vegetables are served whole and can be sliced up to accompany small bowls of hummus, *babaghanoush* and other dips. And in many areas of the Levant, in anticipation of a meal of hummus, a dish of pickles in salt brine and small, bitter olives are placed on the table alongside fresh flatbreads.

Traditionally, hummus can be served as one of many small dishes – including salads, cheeses and little savoury pastries – or else as a substantial meal in its own right. In the first instance it may be an appetizer served as part of a larger meal,

Fluffy Turkish bread topped with sesame seeds and nigella seeds is a delicious accompaniment to hummus.

usually one of many vegetarian precursors to a main meal of meat. The food writer and nutritionist Nada Saleh recalls the picnics of her childhood in the Lebanese mountains, where the family would enjoy a traditional meze spread of hummus, *tabouleh*, *labneh* (strained yoghurt), olives and bread followed by *kibbe* and grilled meats.[8]

In the second instance, a bowl of fresh hummus provides a hearty but modest breakfast or lunch when served alongside vegetables and bread. This kind of meal is available in small, simple restaurants specializing in hummus (in Israel such a restaurant is known as a *hummusiya*). Hummus and falafel also make for a popular homemade breakfast in many Levantine countries, often enjoyed on a Friday morning to mark the beginning of the weekend. Furthermore, the combination of hummus and falafel is a filling and inexpensive combination (unlike meat-based meals): whether eaten out or prepared at home, it is food to feed the family. As the Palestinian journalist Mousa Tawfiq remarks, this 'rich and affordable meal' can

Hummus in the Levant is often eaten as part of a selection of meze.

Hummus and falafel, served on a plate or in a flatbread with salads and sauces, is a popular combination across the Levant.

be eaten all year round, served with a cold juice in summer and a hot tea in winter.[9]

Despite widespread adherence to the simple chickpea-tahini-lemon-garlic formula, even the traditionally prepared hummus of the eastern Mediterranean can come with a twist or two. Rather than adding flavours to the hummus itself, Levantine cuisine tends to favour topping the hummus with extra ingredients, creating simple variations on the classic recipe. The traditional manner of serving hummus, spread round the hollow of a small red clay bowl, lends itself to the addition of other ingredients that bring contrasts in colour, flavour and texture. In Levantine cuisine there are a number of favourite ways of embellishing a bowl of hummus.

First and foremost: olive oil. Perhaps the only topping that cannot be dispensed with, olive oil is a vital ingredient in Mediterranean cuisine and an essential flavour on the Levantine hummus plate (though it should not be mixed into the hummus itself – water is used for thinning). Olive oil may be used in combination with any other topping for hummus. It is added liberally, enough to fill the hollow in the hummus bowl, so that the bread used for dipping in the hummus is likewise soaked in oil. A greenish olive oil with a good, punchy flavour is generally used for this task. A final sprinkle of paprika is a very common addition, and adds a dash of colour to the hummus as well as a gentle bite.

Second, across the Levant one of the most popular ways of serving hummus is to top the dish with its central ingredients: a light, lemony tahini (made by thinning the sesame paste with water and lemon juice) or a scattering of whole chickpeas, which are set aside before the rest are puréed into hummus. The chickpeas bring a welcome contrast of textures, while the added tahini gives the dish a creamier overall flavour.

Third, as is popular in Egypt and elsewhere, a flavoursome stew or paste of fava beans known as *ful* may be served in the centre of a dish of hummus. The combination of pulses yields an even heartier and more substantial meal (one is famously sleepy all afternoon after a lunch of *ful*). In Egypt these same fava beans are the staple ingredient of *ta'miyya*, the Egyptian version of the classic Levantine chickpea-based falafel. But fava beans are equally popular in the Levant. Abu Hassan, a famous hummus restaurant in Jaffa, serves a dish of hummus with three classic toppings, *ful*, tahini and chickpeas, which is known as a *meshulash* (meaning 'triangle' in Hebrew).

Fourth, hummus in the Levant may be served with a topping of lamb or beef – either ground or very finely sliced – cooked with spices and perhaps garnished with pine nuts. Another variation is to top the hummus with slices of *sujuk*, a spicy sausage generally made from beef. Traditionally speaking, hummus is a simple vegetarian dish and the use of meat thus elevates it to something more extravagant. For this reason,

Fava beans, known in Arabic as *ful*, make a popular addition to the hummus plate.

the addition of meat to hummus is more common where the dish stands as part of a selection of elegantly served meze – simple eateries serving larger portions of hummus designed to constitute a whole meal are more often vegetarian.

Fifth, hummus in Israel is very frequently topped with a quartered hard-boiled egg – often in combination with tahini and whole chickpeas. This hearty combination is usually served with a small portion of *zhug*: a fiery green condiment brought to Israel by Yemenite Jews, made with chillies, coriander, parsley, garlic, olive oil and spices. While hard-boiled eggs are a popular breakfast food across the Middle East, Israelis often incorporate them into simple street foods as well. Hard-boiled eggs are an essential ingredient of Israeli *sabih* (a pitta filled with slices of aubergine, potato and egg and garnished with tahini, salads and *amba*, a strongly flavoured mango pickle), and Israelis also use hard-boiled eggs to accompany savoury pastries known as *bourekas*, which are commonly filled with cheese, potato or spinach.

Sixth, parsley, which is commonly sprinkled over a dish of hummus as a final garnish, may also be finely chopped and added into the hummus at the time of mixing, flecking the smooth hummus with tiny pieces of green herb. This version, a Lebanese speciality, is often known as *hummus beiruti* (Beirut hummus). Parsley is also the central ingredient of the Levantine *tabouleh*, a finely chopped herb, vegetable and cracked-wheat salad that often accompanies hummus as part of a meze spread.

And finally, a warm variation of hummus known as *mus-abbaha* (literally meaning 'swimming' in Arabic) is a favourite in the Levant, though it is virtually unheard of in the West. In some areas this same dish is known as *mashawsha* ('jumbled up'). *Musabbaha* uses the same ingredients as hummus, but in a somewhat deconstructed fashion. In this variation most of the chickpeas are left whole, the garlicky, lemony tahini providing a kind of sauce (cumin and parsley are popular additions to this dish). Unlike hummus, which is commonly served at room temperature, *musabbaha* is eaten warm for breakfast or lunch, accompanied by bread and pickles as classic hummus would be.

The traditional eastern Mediterranean methods of preparing and serving hummus thus do little to stray from the classic recipe. Across the Near and Middle East, people continue to enjoy hummus as it has been made for centuries, seeking high-quality versions of the original dish rather than any kind of innovation in its preparation and recipe. This kind of fidelity to the original recipe is not unusual – many cuisines worldwide display a reluctance to tamper with long-established favourite dishes. What's more, all of the traditional embellishments discussed above have undoubtedly found

Musabbaha, a kind of deconstructed hummus, is a favourite Levantine breakfast.

their way onto the hummus plate by virtue of being foods that were frequently served alongside hummus. Meat, parsley, fava beans – all of these naturally belong at the table with hummus in the guises of *kofta*, *tabouleh* and *ful* (among other dishes). But no additions are found that go beyond the typical flavours of a meze spread or a Middle Eastern breakfast.

Back home in the heartlands of this delicious chickpea and tahini dip, there are pumpkins and lentils for hearty winter soups and stews but no pumpkin and lentil hummus. In the same way, Middle Eastern patisserie caters to the very sweet-toothed, yet there is no local market for dessert hummus, sweetened with a rich sugar syrup. There is, however, a significant market for freshly made hummus: prepared, served and eaten on the same day. Although tubs of hummus are available to purchase in supermarkets across the eastern Mediterranean (as they are across much of the rest of the world), people also continue to go out to enjoy fresh hummus – as an appetizer or as a wholesome main meal. Shop-bought hummus certainly pales in comparison to the real stuff. And as such, these are the defining features of hummus as it is traditionally made – its quality, simplicity and freshness, as well as its ability to take centre stage.

3
Spreading the Hummus

Though hummus as we know it today had long been enjoyed across the eastern Mediterranean region, it remained largely unknown in the Western world until the second half of the twentieth century. Cosmopolitan neighbourhoods in European and American cities were initially introduced to hummus in this period through Mediterranean eateries, including Greek, Turkish and Lebanese restaurants. Many such establishments were founded across the world by Middle Eastern cooks and chefs who had fled political unrest (including the Lebanese Civil War) and economic uncertainty. Restaurants such as these initially served mostly immigrant communities, offering up traditional Middle Eastern and Mediterranean cuisine to those longing for the flavours of home. Over time, however, the scents and flavours of Middle Eastern cooking trickled over into Western food culture, which itself had increasingly begun to look outwards for culinary inspiration.

At the same time, growing vegetarian movements in the West in the latter part of the twentieth century embraced hummus as a nutritious, wholesome, meat-free food. For this reason, like a plate of brown rice and dal, hummus also developed a reputation as a hippie food – it was served at cafés and restaurants catering for a new wave of vegetarians. But the number of hummus-eaters in the West remained low: these early encounters had little effect on the way most Europeans and North Americans ate on a daily basis. Hummus remained confined to Mediterranean delis and vegetarian cafés, and was certainly not eaten by the average European or American at home.

By the turn of the twenty-first century, however, hummus had become a global phenomenon, eaten in vast quantities across the United States, Australia, Europe and elsewhere. Of all the European markets, none has embraced hummus so wholeheartedly as that of the British. More than 40 per cent of British consumers have a tub of hummus in their fridge, a figure nearly double that of their European neighbours.[1] This equates to a British consumption of some 12,000 tonnes of hummus a year, fuelling an industry worth more than £60

Hummus has become a hugely popular snack food, sold in supermarkets across the West.

million.[2] But how did hummus become so popular with the British in such a short space of time?

Writing in her debut work, *A Book of Mediterranean Food*, in 1955, Elizabeth David was the first author to bring hummus to an English-language cookbook. She calls her recipe for *hummus bi-tahina* 'an Egyptian version of an Arab dish' and even explains to her readers what tahini is and where to find it, suggesting three London outlets that stock Mediterranean ingredients.[3] She further explains that tahini mixed with oil, water and garlic may be eaten as a little dish itself when served with bread for dipping. Unusually, David's recipe for hummus also calls for olive oil and mint (either fresh or dried). As a guide, David instructs her reader to mix the hummus to the consistency of a 'thick mayonnaise', using a product her readers would all have been familiar with to describe something relatively unknown. She proposes pouring the hummus into a large serving dish or onto individual saucers but does not suggest a particular garnish or accompaniment.

Elizabeth David was born and raised in Britain but spent many years living and travelling in France, Greece and Egypt, from which she drew inspiration for her writing. On her return to Britain in 1946 she discovered a culinary culture stifled by the restrictions of Second World War food rationing. The ingredients her recipes called for, such as olive oil and figs, were by no means readily available in post-war Britain. However, her descriptions of exotic and flavoursome dishes resonated with the British public, and her work played an influential role in the dramatic changes that British food underwent in the following decades. *A Book of Mediterranean Food* is today considered one of the classics of culinary literature.

In many ways Elizabeth David set the stage for perhaps the most influential Mediterranean food writer of the twentieth century, Claudia Roden, whose *Book of Middle Eastern Food* was first published in 1968. This work likewise contains a recipe for *hummus bi-tahina*, which Roden describes as the tahini salad 'most widely known and appreciated of all outside the Middle East'.[4] She recommends serving the hummus as an appetiser, or with 'bread, fish, aubergines – practically anything'. While Elizabeth David categorizes her hummus under 'Cold Foods and Salads', Claudia Roden uses the term 'Hors D'Oeuvre'. Both descriptions attempt to give the Western reader in the 1950s and '60s an insight into the Mediterranean meze culture to which hummus naturally belongs.

In the traditional fashion, Roden's recipe calls for dried chickpeas (120–180 grams (4–6 oz), soaked overnight), the juice of two to three lemons (or to taste), two to three cloves of garlic, salt and tahini. She suggests pressing the cooked chickpeas through a sieve or pounding them in a mortar – or preferably using a blender or electric mixer to achieve a smooth purée. Like Elizabeth David, she uses mayonnaise to describe the desired consistency of hummus. Roden also suggests a final garnish of olive oil, paprika and finely chopped parsley.

Unlike Elizabeth David, Claudia Roden drew on her own roots in researching and collecting Middle Eastern and Mediterranean recipes. Born in Cairo to parents of Syrian Jewish origin, she moved to Paris in her late teens and later studied and settled in London. Like that of David, Roden's work should also be read as a reaction to the unadventurous nature of mid-century British cuisine (which was, as she describes it, 'horrifyingly bad').[5] In Roden's case her writing recounted favourite dishes from the cosmopolitan Egypt of her childhood as well as recipes she sourced from knowledgeable family members and friends.

Following in these footsteps, a number of other food writers specializing in Mediterranean and Middle Eastern

Street scene in Cairo, 1950, photographed by Willem van de Poll.

cuisine began to emerge over the course of the late twentieth century. Though there was interest, the market for this kind of literature was not yet discerning. The American writers Joan Nathan and Judy Stacey Goldman provide one recipe for hummus in their cookbook *The Flavor of Jerusalem*, published in the United States in 1974. This recipe not only recommends the usage of canned chickpeas but advises readers to serve the dish 'well chilled'.[6] As far as Middle Eastern and Mediterranean food is concerned, the best-known food writer of this century is the Israeli author and chef Yotam Ottolenghi. Like Claudia Roden before him, Ottolenghi does not merely present recipes as lists of ingredients and instructions; he delves into a fuller picture of the foods he describes, reflecting, reminiscing and telling stories. In light of the fact that his twenty-first-century Western audience was already familiar with this cuisine, Ottolenghi took a different approach, sparking a trend for a new kind of Middle Eastern food: one that is playful, inventive and focused on putting vegetables centre stage. This has been explored through his London delis and restaurants, his cookbooks, and also through his popular weekly column in *The Guardian*, 'The New Vegetarian'. When it comes to hummus, however, Ottolenghi remains faithful to the traditional ingredients and preparation. The recipe he gives in his hugely successful cookbook *Jerusalem* (2012) is for classic, high-quality Levantine hummus. He does not intend to inform the reader what hummus is – hummus is already ubiquitous on supermarket shelves and in our fridges, of course – but rather what real, freshly made hummus can be.

In addition to being introduced to hummus through food writing and Mediterranean cuisine at home, the general increase in travel and tourism in the 1960s and '70s brought with it exposure to new foods and flavours. A family holiday to Greece exposed people to dishes previously unknown, such as spanakopita, moussaka and hummus. By the 1980s British supermarkets were attempting to bring some of these exciting and exotic flavours into people's own homes, and in 1988 the upmarket chain Waitrose launched the first pre-packaged pots of hummus in the UK.[7] Within a few years a number of other supermarkets had followed suit, stocking hummus alongside a selection of increasingly popular dips. But while supermarket-made taramasalata and guacamole enjoyed moderate popularity, hummus was received with unprecedented enthusiasm.

Writing in *The Guardian* in 2017, Felicity Cloake remarked that hummus 'didn't go really mainstream until the mid-1990s, when, along with exotica such as sun-dried tomatoes and pesto, it came to represent the cosmopolitan sunny optimism of New Labour'.[8] In the space of around thirty years, hummus has moved from being an exotic and occasional treat to a British supermarket essential. Indeed, when a production issue causing a strange metallic flavour required several UK supermarkets (including Marks & Spencer and Sainsbury's) to withdraw their hummus from supermarket shelves the shortage was labelled the 2017 'hummus crisis'. Distressed customers took to Twitter and other social-media platforms, venting their intense frustration at being unable to purchase their regular tub of hummus. Incidentally, the hummus crisis also revealed that the international food manufacturer Bakkavor was responsible for the centralized production of a great number of supermarket own-brand dips, including hummus. For this reason, pots of hummus were affected across the country, and across the full super-market spectrum.

A number of factors may have contributed to the unparalleled popularity of hummus in the UK and elsewhere. First, it tastes delicious. When made well, hummus strikes a wonderful balance of flavours – garlicky, lemony and creamy all at once. It also tastes delicious with almost everything, which cannot be said of many foods. Second, unlike many snack foods, it has a wholesome, healthy image – no doubt in part owing to its association with vegetarianism and Mediterranean food. While vegetarianism has always been perceived as being wholesome, Mediterranean food has relatively recently risen to prominence as being one of the healthiest cuisines, rich in fruit, vegetables, grains, pulses and olive oil. And hummus's healthy image is wholly justified: it is a great source of protein, soluble fibres, healthy fats, B vitamins and folic acid, and essential minerals such as folate, magnesium, potassium and calcium. It ranks low on the glycaemic index, keeping you feeling full for longer. Hummus also contains high levels of tryptophan, an amino acid known for its numerous health benefits and for improving our general mood. Healthy and delicious is a winning combination.

Third, being based on the humble chickpea, hummus is relatively inexpensive. A pot or two of supermarket hummus (usually sold in portions of between 150 and 300 grams, or 5 to 10 ounces) makes only a moderate dent on the shopping bill. Since chickpeas are stored either dried or cooked (and tinned) after being harvested they are readily available all year around: hummus is thus not season dependent. Homemade hummus made from dried or tinned chickpeas is, of course, even cheaper than shop-bought. Although hummus was initially launched by an upmarket chain, most British supermarkets today stock a range of varieties of hummus, of which at least one will be presented as a simple, highly affordable option. Nonetheless, the majority of hummus consumers in the UK

Although supermarket hummus is a relatively affordable food item, hummus made at home using dried chickpeas is invariably cheaper (and more delicious).

are middle class, and hummus has become a day-to-day food predominantly for this social group.[9]

Fourth, hummus is a great convenience food. A pot of hummus in the fridge at home (or at work) is an instant healthy snack, almost invariably eaten straight from its packaging with raw vegetables, pitta or another dipping food of choice. And finally, hummus is extremely versatile. As much a spread as a dip, hummus has been adopted as a sandwich filling – both as base layer, in the manner of butter, mayonnaise or cream cheese, and primary filling, when accompanied by ingredients such as falafel or roasted vegetables. It can be served to friends as an appetizer while dinner is cooking, or alongside sticks of carrot and cucumber at a children's party, or nestled among the quiches and scotch eggs of a summery picnic spread. Not to mention that quintessential British combination, served anytime and anywhere: hummus and crisps.

Similarly, on the other side of the Atlantic, North America was initially introduced to hummus on a small scale through the Mediterranean restaurants established by its immigrant population in the twentieth century. It likewise witnessed a wave of enthusiasm for hummus at the turn of the twenty-first century, with most Americans having previously had little exposure to the food. Today around a quarter of all American households are believed to have hummus in the fridge. To meet the growing demand American farmers have vastly increased their chickpea production, yielding around four times the amount they did only a decade ago.[10] Furthermore, American companies have also sought increases in chickpea production by investing in agricultural developments in countries such as Ethiopia.

In the case of America, the initial dramatic rise in popularity had much to do with strategic marketing: hummus was introduced in such a way as to complement the American

Field of chickpea plants in Israel.

lifestyle and way of eating. The hummus market was first dominated by Sabra, a brand launched in 1986 in New York and later acquired by Strauss Group and PepsiCo. Sabra specifically advertised hummus as a cultural movement – bringing it to an American market receptive to new food experiences (and particularly to food experiences that did not depart dramatically from established American eating habits).[11] Hummus, as a creamy dip that could be eaten as a snack food, was a clear winner, and even became the official dip of the National Football League in 2013. As Deb Perelman notes, far from considering it the basis of a full meal, Americans think of hummus as 'a cold snack, a dip you buy in the fridge case to help distract you from, say, cool ranch potato chip dip or something'.[12] According to the USA Dry Pea and Lentil Council, supermarket sales of hummus account for some $725 million each year (twenty years ago this figure was closer to $5 million).[13]

Beyond the United States and Europe, hummus today is known and eaten across the globe. Levantine Arab immigrants (especially the Lebanese) brought their cuisine to the major urban areas of Canada, South America, Australia, the Gulf States and elsewhere in the Middle East. Arab countries that have no history of making hummus have adopted it in the same wave as the rest of the world. In more recent years the Israeli diaspora have also begun to open hummus restaurants in cities around the globe, popularizing the dish even further. Though it has yet to appear universally in supermarkets across the world, hummus can nonetheless be enjoyed globally in restaurants. From Mexico City to Bangkok to Tokyo, there is always somewhere to eat hummus.

But rather than the dishes of freshly made *hummus bi-tahina* that have graced Lebanese meze tables across the world, it is the pre-packaged supermarket version of hummus that has really taken the West by storm. The enthusiasm for hummus as a dip and a spread has been unparalleled in the world of healthy snacking and convenience food. Sales of hummus are expected to rise over the next four years, in line with the planned introduction of new products, novel hummus-making technologies and the growth of hummus sales in emerging markets. However, it remains to be seen what effects the COVID-19 pandemic will have on the production and export of hummus and hummus ingredients – and by extension on global hummus sales. Predicted sales figures may need to be revised in the light of recent changes to the world economy.

The current top manufacturers of pre-packaged hummus are (for the most part) major Israeli, American and European food producers. These producers include Strauss Group (one of the largest food manufacturers in Israel), Tribe Hummus (owned by the Israeli food manufacturer Osem, which in turn belongs to the Nestlé conglomerate) and Athenos (an American company owned by Kraft foods). Other major hummus producers include Bakkavor (an international company that supplies fresh foods, famously the supplier behind the 2017 hummus crisis), Boar's Head (an American supplier of deli meats and cheeses), Lantana Foods and Hope Foods (American companies specializing in different varieties and flavours of hummus), Finnish Cheese Company, Cedar's (an American company supplying Mediterranean dips and salads), Sevan AB (a Swedish brand) and Vermont Hummus Company.

Major hummus manufacturers such as these produce a wide range of hummus flavours, but it is the 'original', red pepper, garlic, black olive and white bean in particular that dominate the hummus market. Smaller manufacturers, which often supply independent shops and produce hummus for the organic market, also rely on their diverse range of flavours as a major selling point. The Precious Pea, a hummus company based in Tunley (just outside Bath), market their selection of hummus dips on the basis of their high-quality, organic ingredients and the overall improvement in flavour that comes with using these superior ingredients. Nonetheless, the flavours of hummus that they have created (such as beetroot, kalamata and rose harissa) are remarkably similar to those made by the large-scale manufacturers. Furthermore, like most supermarket hummus, the Precious Pea version also contains oil (though in this case better-tasting extra virgin olive oil replaces the more commonly used sunflower or rapeseed oil). To a certain extent, then, even the higher-quality versions of pre-packaged hummus rely on the typical supermarket-style formula.

Pre-packaged hummus is sold today in supermarkets across the world, with major sales in countries that span six continents. However, this global love affair with hummus has, in many ways, soured the subject back home in the Levant. As the world consumes more and more of this creamy chick-pea dip, the big Levantine players have quickly scrambled to call it their own.

Poster for *Hummus! The Movie* (2015), directed by Oren Rosenfeld.

4
War and Peas

While hummus has gained in popularity across the world, and especially over the course of the last twenty or thirty years, back home in the Levant it has become an increasingly contentious subject. From competitions to produce the largest single serving of hummus to attempts to claim hummus as authentically the food of one cuisine or another, this intense competition has been dubbed the 'hummus wars'. And this is before we even consider the fierce rivalry between neighbouring hummus restaurants in any given town or city in the Levantine region. Customers' allegiance to one hummus restaurant or another in this context may be compared to that which is reserved for sports teams in other parts of the world. Loving hummus, it seems, means also having to fight over it.

The competition to create the Guinness World Records' largest dish of hummus began in May 2008 in Jerusalem. Under the sponsorship of Tzabar (an Israeli food company), a number of chefs prepared some 400 kg (880 lb) of hummus, claiming the record for themselves. In response, a group of chefs in Lebanon produced a dish of hummus weighing in at over 2,055 kg (4,530 lb). Israel responded to this with a 4,079-kilogram (8,993 lb) serving, produced in the Arab-Israeli village of Abu Ghosh under the supervision of Jawdat Ibrahim. But on 8 May 2010 the current world record was claimed by the Lebanese chef Ramzi Choueiri, alongside three hundred student chefs at the Al-Kafaat University in Beirut. Together they produced 10,452 kg (23,042 lb) of hummus, served on a ceramic plate measuring 7.17 m (23½ ft) in diameter that had been specially made for the occasion by a local architect. This bowl of hummus was decorated with the image of a cedar: the Lebanese national symbol.

This competition has taken place in the wake of political tensions: Israel and Lebanon have fought two wars in the last forty years, the first in 1982 and the second in 2006. However, it must also be seen as part of the greater struggle to claim 'ownership' over hummus: a nationalistic conflict. The historian Ari Ariel has compared the strong expression of nationalism involved in culinary competitions to that of sporting events such as the Olympics.[1] Certainly the strong image of the cedar on Lebanon's winning bowl of hummus

The Guinness World Records's largest dish of hummus was created on 8 May 2010 by Lebanese chef Ramzi Choueiri and 300 student chefs.

indicated that this was a national victory. Furthermore, from the Lebanese perspective, the desire to win the hummus wars is intertwined with the desire to claim exclusive ownership of hummus, presenting it to the world as a solely Lebanese national food.

From the Israeli perspective, however, competing to create the largest dish of hummus is representative of the wish to be seen as the most prominent hummus-makers of our times. Israel has become a hugely successful exporter of hummus, and has done much to contribute to its global popularity in recent years (Lebanese products, on the other hand, are not as widely consumed worldwide).

The Guinness World Records competition was discussed and documented in the Israeli-made 2015 film *Hummus! The Movie*. This film looks at the lives and work of three hummus-makers in Israel and Palestine: one Muslim, one Christian and one Jewish. Hummus has also featured on the screen in the Australian-made *Make Hummus Not War*, released in 2012. This film addresses hummus politics: the various claims to its ownership and the resulting hummus conflicts. Indeed, where hummus appears in popular culture today its story is very often intertwined with the politics of the Levantine region.

But Israeli claims to being the original hummus-makers are few and far between (with the exception of those who have suggested it was a biblical food, preserved for centuries in the land of Israel by the local Arabs). The Israeli relationship with hummus is complex and multilayered. Before the establishment of the state of Israel in 1948 it was eaten in the country then known as Palestine by Jews, Muslims and Christians alike. Furthermore, to a certain extent it was also adopted by early Jewish immigrants to Palestine, alongside falafel, chopped vegetable salads, pitta and other local foods. One early twentieth-century account of the Castel family

– a Jewish family of Spanish descent – describes their home in Jerusalem, including a table set with hummus and tahini.[2]

In an attempt to change eating habits, various Jewish organizations recommended that Jewish immigrants to Palestine adopt the local cuisine. This recommendation was made primarily on two fronts: practicality and ideology. From a practical perspective, early Jewish immigrants were encouraged to adapt their tastes and learn to cook local foods because those were the ones most readily available. It was far more affordable to learn to prepare local vegetarian dishes based on regional ingredients than it was to source the more familiar flavours of the kitchens they had left behind. For European Jews, this meant tackling unfamiliar ingredients and adapting their cooking styles and repertoires. From an ideological perspective, adapting tastes and eating habits was also interconnected with the Zionist movement that sought reinvention in the land of Israel. This movement was reflected in the revival of Hebrew as a language for Jews in the land of Israel, and in the introduction of a new way of eating based on local foods – especially foods that could be grown and cultivated in the land.

After the establishment of the state of Israel in 1948, Jewish Israelis were further exposed to hummus (and other Levantine foods) through two different channels. On the one hand, they began to eat more frequently at Palestinian restaurants in Arab towns, where they could avoid the state rationing system. On the other hand, the establishment of the state of Israel brought waves of Jewish immigrants from the surrounding Middle Eastern countries. Some Arab Jews, including Syrians and Egyptians, were already hummus-eaters, and continued to prepare and serve hummus in Israel. Many other eastern Jews, however, began serving hummus in their restaurants in Israel because it was popular, rather than because they

A simple meal in the dining hall of Kibbutz Maabarot in 1939, photographed by Zoltan Kluger.

had once eaten it at home. Hummus in Israel was thus somewhat disconnected from its Palestinian roots and rebranded as a Middle Eastern Jewish-Israeli food.

Over time hummus increased in popularity in Israel, and today Israelis consider it a beloved national food. Only in more recent years has there been a surge of enthusiasm for celebrating hummus as Arab, and for according Arab hummus in Israel particular 'gourmet' status. In commenting on the Israeli–Lebanese hummus battle, the Israeli celebrity chef Haim Cohen has stated that 'it's not the Israelis in Israel that are doing the hummus, it's the Arabs.'[3] Cohen's description presents hummus in this particular context as belonging to the realm of Arab-Israeli food culture rather than Jewish-Israeli. (Arab-Israelis should not be confused with Arab-Jews: the former are Arabic-speaking Muslim and Christian citizens of the state of Israel, while the latter are Jews of Arab origin or heritage). According to Ari Ariel, this new perspective on hummus culture has come about as hummus has been fully naturalized in Israel, giving Israelis a new position from which to examine and reflect on its culinary roots.[4]

In many ways the Israeli way of serving and eating hummus serves as a bridge between Levantine tradition and Western innovation. While Israelis have embraced the Levantine method of preparing hummus according to the classic recipe and the custom of eating it as a sustaining morning or lunchtime meal – with pitta, salads and pickles on the side – they are also large consumers (and producers) of pre-packaged hummus. Israel began producing hummus on an industrial scale in the 1950s, and from then the market has grown at an unprecedented rate. While Israeli pre-packaged hummus is widely consumed in Israeli households, it is also extremely popular with the European and u.s. markets: Strauss Group, for example, is an Israeli company that continues to be a major player in the European and American hummus markets.

Israelis are also often creative in embellishing hummus with adventurous toppings. Many Israeli hummus restaurants, though by and large ones outside of Israel, serve hummus topped with mushrooms, sliced aubergines, *shakshuka* (a flavoursome dish of cooked tomatoes and peppers topped with an egg) and many other things besides. Far from serving hummus in the traditional clay bowl, such restaurants offer it any way they like – even stacked in tiers to form a multicoloured hummus trio: one classic, one brilliant pink and beetroot flavoured, and another pale green, mixed with mashed avocado.

These unorthodox methods of serving hummus may be partly designed to appeal to the Western consumer: hummus in Israel is generally more traditional, and high-quality classic hummus is prized over anything more innovative. Furthermore, within Israel, Arab-Israeli hummus-makers are regarded as the masters of the trade (as Haim Cohen's comment indicates). But the use of mushrooms, beetroot and avocado also reflects the often playful nature of Israeli food, which itself constitutes a blend of many more traditional cuisines – most prominent among them the local Palestinian cuisine that gave rise to a national love of hummus and falafel. It is this eclectic combination of different cuisines that yields dishes and flavour combinations which break with tradition, creating a new cuisine that uses the best elements of each food culture: hummus, yes, but also Yemenite breads such as *kubaneh* and *jachnun*, as well as the rich, sweet babkas of the Ashkenazi kitchen.

Lebanon has even gone beyond hummus-making competitions in pursuit of ownership of hummus. In 2008 the Association of Lebanese Industrialists (ALI) began their 'Hands Off Our Dishes' campaign, with the intention of formally registering a number of Levantine dishes with the

Israeli hummus restaurants often offer unusual toppings, such as mushrooms or shakshuka.

European Union as Lebanese products. Among these dishes was that globally beloved creamy dip: hummus. Registering hummus as a Lebanese product would have given Lebanon exclusive rights over the name 'hummus' and required that all other hummus producers market their product under a different name. The EU has accorded such status to particular traditional products since 1992 in an effort to protect their specific names and ensure their quality. The status is granted on the basis of either traditional preparation methods or else the specific geographical location in which at least one stage of the production is carried out. In 2002, for example, Greece won the rights to the name 'feta', meaning that non-Greek feta-like cheeses could not be marketed under that name. If the Lebanese campaign had been successful, all other hummus producers would have been exporting 'chickpea dip', 'garbanzo smash' or some other such unlikely-sounding product.

This Lebanese campaign was undoubtedly aimed at Israel: it forms a further episode in the ongoing Lebanese–Israeli hummus wars. The common consumption of particular foods has always been strongly tied to the construction of community identity and, by extension, to the imagined separation of 'us' from 'them'. In claiming hummus as a Lebanese food, ALI identified the Lebanese as the 'authentic' hummus-eaters, in contrast with Israelis, whose culture ALI depicted as being predominantly European. Indeed, the president of ALI, Fadi Abboud, has remarked of Israel's hummus culture: 'with all due respect, I didn't know German Jews or Polish Jews knew anything about hummus.'[5]

The attempt to make hummus exclusively Lebanese must therefore be viewed as an attempt to stop hummus from being considered an Israeli food on an international scale. And while underlying political tensions must surely have contributed to the actions of ALI, Israel's comparative success in exporting hummus must also be taken into account as a strong motivating factor. Abboud has also specifically stated: 'if we eat Sabra hummus, the very popular [Israeli] hummus available in UK supermarkets, there is no mention of Lebanon anywhere on the package. They call it an Israeli traditional dish, for heaven's sake.'[6] It is interesting to note that this latter claim is not actually at all well founded. Israeli hummus is rarely marketed as being Israeli and is more often described as a Mediterranean food. As Ari Ariel notes, this description may reflect the major Israeli food companies' wish to avoid labelling (and acknowledging) hummus as being an Arab food.[7] At the same time, it may illustrate their attempts to promote hummus further by aligning it with the wholesome, healthy image of the Mediterranean diet. In my opinion, marketing the hummus as being 'Mediterranean' rather than 'Israeli' may also be an intentional means of attracting consumers who, for political reasons, would find off-putting negative connotations in the description 'Israeli'.

Needless to say, the Lebanese campaign to trademark hummus was unsuccessful. Hummus, as a food widely eaten across a relatively large region (representing a number of different states), does not fit the criteria of a trademarked and registered food product. Although the campaign was aimed at Israel, it would also have prevented Palestinian, Syrian and Jordanian companies from exporting and marketing a product they called 'hummus'. It is helpful to remember that the dish known as *hummus bi-tahina* certainly pre-dates the nation-states in which it is eaten today. If hummus was indeed first prepared for the eighteenth-century rulers of Damascus or Beirut then it was perhaps initially a food of the urban centres of the Ottoman Empire, rather than one of Syria or Lebanon as we think of them today.

As Yotam Ottolenghi has reflected in *Jerusalem* (2012), debates over the ownership of food are essentially futile.[8] As he notes, they are ultimately irrelevant (because food and eating belong firmly to the present moment), never-ending (because every new dish has its precursory dishes) and ambiguous (because food culture does not develop in a vacuum – every cuisine is necessarily subject to numerous influences through travel, trade and other forms of interaction). To this end, he gives the following remarks on the 'ownership' of hummus:

> Hummus, for example, a highly explosive subject, is undeniably a staple of the local Palestinian population, but it was also a permanent feature on the dinner tables of Allepian [*sic*] Jews who have lived in Syria for millennia and then arrived in Jerusalem in the 1950s and 1960s. Who is more deserving of calling hummus their own? Neither. Nobody 'owns' a dish because it is very likely that someone else cooked it before them and another person before that.[9]

However, although record-breaking plates of hummus and international disputes of ownership are what make the news, there are other kinds hummus wars too – ones played out on a daily basis. In Levantine towns and cities, where freshly made hummus is widely eaten and appreciated, everyone has their favourite hummus restaurant, and debates over which of these produces the best hummus quickly become heated arguments. Everyone prefers their hummus a little differently, and these minor details can be the source of lengthy discussions simply because hummus really is that important. Diala Shaheen, author of the food blog 'The Hummus Theory' (which represents the intersection of Palestinian cuisine and healthy eating), remarks: 'My passion for hummus is unreasonable. Is it the chickpeas, is it the tahini, or just how good they go together? It doesn't matter.'[10]

Those who make hummus know exactly how closely it is scrutinized by their customers, dedicating themselves to perfecting their own recipe and manner of serving. Everything from the raw ingredients to the cooking style and seasoning will affect the final results. As Ariel Rosenthal, the Israeli chef and restaurant owner, has described it, 'Like the polishing of a diamond, hummus requires work – perfecting, sharpening, and refining.'[11] For those who really love hummus – whether making it or eating it – it is so much more than a dip. As Rosenthal himself puts it: 'The chickpea is my world.'[12]

The great irony of the conflict that surrounds hummus is that it has the potential to be the ultimate uniting food in the Middle East. First off, it is hugely popular, and as such it's eaten and enjoyed across the region irrespective of religion, class, gender, age group or ethnicity (albeit with minor differences in preparation and serving style according to geographical location). Second, hummus, as a plant-based food, is not governed by the restrictions of the religious dietary laws and practices that shape the eating habits of the Muslims, Christians and Jews of the Middle East and eastern Mediterranean. Muslim and Jewish dietary laws only prohibit the consumption of certain kinds of meat, and require that the slaughter of animals fit for food is halal or kosher respectively. In addition, Jews are forbidden from consuming meat with milk and other dairy products. As mentioned in the first chapter, many denominations of Middle Eastern Christians abstain from meat, fish, dairy and eggs during fasting days such as Lent. Hummus, being based on entirely vegetal ingredients, is thus suitable for all diets and all communities.

Make Hummus Not Walls graffiti on the West Bank barrier in Bethlehem.

Third, hummus is food to bring people together: when eaten as part of a meze, it is a dish designed to be shared among many. Breaking and dipping bread is a highly social activity – be it into dishes of *labneh* (strained yoghurt, often topped with olive oil and a spice mix known as *za'atar*), *mutabbal* (a mixture of puréed burnt aubergine and tahini) or *hummus bi-tahina*. Middle Eastern culture attaches great importance to the act of sharing food, associating with it the strong bonds that are forged over the dinner table.

Jawdat Ibrahim, the Arab-Israeli chef who competed with Lebanon in attempting to claim the record for the largest dish of hummus, has a particularly optimistic wish that hummus might one day bring the whole region together. He states: 'I am saying to people in Lebanon, Syria, Jordan, and Egypt: I know the situation is complicated because there is no peace, but I would love it to happen one day, that we can cook one plate of hummus – about 10,000 tons – to share with the whole Middle East.'[13] The essence of this vision is bright and hopeful in acknowledging the common fondness for this chickpea dip. Sharing hummus, and a love for hummus, is rife with opportunity for uniting people.

Buddha bowls often feature hummus alongside other wholesome, plant-based foods.

5
Generation Hummus

Today hummus is truly a global food, eaten in Mediterranean and Middle Eastern restaurants across the world. What's more, in the West it has become an ordinary, everyday food, bought in supermarkets, served in pubs and cafés, and stocked in home fridges. In many UK café chains, a sandwich spread with hummus feels as familiar and commonplace today as one spread with chutney or mayonnaise. Like aubergines, peppers and other Mediterranean flavours, hummus has lost its 'exotic' status and become absorbed into the twenty-first-century way of eating in the West, in which popularized dishes from all cuisines are readily available from mainstream shops and eateries. In being absorbed, hummus has undergone a Western makeover, yielding a hummus culture quite different from that of the Levantine region. What's more, in becoming an everyday food 'hummus' has become a general descriptive term: all manner of dips and pastes made from vegetables and pulses now come under the broad umbrella of 'hummus'.

As quickly as it was embraced in Europe and the United States (in the space of the last thirty years or so), hummus became a repetitive format: chickpeas, tahini, garlic and lemon on repeat. Pre-packaged supermarket pots of hummus also contain vegetable oil (usually rapeseed or sunflower) and accordingly have a lower proportion of tahini to chickpeas, but the essential flavours remain the same. As with crisps and other snack foods, the Western consumer was enticed with diversity in flavour, and a whole range of supermarket hummus varieties was born. In creating new varieties, additional ingredients were added to the traditional hummus flavours – crucially being blended in to enhance the overall flavour rather than added as toppings. In Europe and the United States today it is more or less taken for granted that hummus comes in a number of different flavours. The UK supermarket chain Waitrose offers some eighteen different varieties of hummus, including their own brand of products (both basic and high-end options) and a range of products from popular hummus producers. The selection includes: lemon and spiced apricot; chilli harissa; turmeric (topped with pickled cabbage and pomegranate); beetroot; pea; avocado; red pepper; Moroccan spice; caramelized onion; lemon and coriander; peri-peri; extra virgin olive oil; za'atar; smoked (also with harissa or

Beetroot has become a popular flavour for Western-style hummus.

beetroot); low fat (available in combination with carrot sticks); and baby-led weaning hummus with breadsticks.

This selection provides a good example of the broad spectrum of varieties available, and of the diversity of foods and cuisines that appear today as hummus flavours. Some varieties borrow flavours from Middle Eastern and North African cuisine, including za'atar, harissa and Moroccan spice. Za'atar is, of course, a popular Levantine flavouring, though not one that is often used to flavour hummus in the kitchens of the Levant. Harissa and Moroccan spices naturally belong to the opposite end of the Mediterranean basin, where they form part of a wholly different culinary culture (not one that traditionally serves and eats hummus). Perhaps 'Moroccan' is so often used as an adjective for industrially produced hummus because it conjures up images of exotic and inviting holiday destinations, while the names of Levantine countries are associated with news stories, conflicts and wars.

Other varieties of supermarket hummus simply include vegetables (pea, avocado, red pepper, beetroot), which make for a more colourful and healthier-sounding dip. Smoked hummus perhaps draws its inspiration from *mutabbal*, a Levantine dish of smoked aubergines mashed with tahini, while lemon and coriander is a popular British supermarket flavouring for deli items. Olives, too, are typically available in a lemon and coriander version. The inclusion of peri-peri flavours take hummus in quite a different culinary direction, while low fat (read: low tahini) and baby versions are obviously strategic lifestyle variations. The baby hummus, incidentally, uses no vegetable oil, but it is also made blander (in the way of much pre-prepared baby food) with the omission of garlic. Hummus, as a simple and nutritious purée, is today considered an excellent food for babies and small children. Indeed, in 2013 Penguin Books published Joel Rickett and Spencer Wilson's tongue-in-cheek guide to the essentials of twenty-first-century middle-class family life, entitled *H is for Hummus: A Modern Parent's ABC*.

Over and beyond the varieties of hummus available to buy in the supermarket, yet further iterations exist as recipes in books, on blogs and in many other forms. An Internet search yields recipes for every imaginable flavour of hummus, using any vegetable, spice or herb you can think of. Even Yotam Ottolenghi, who, for the most part, considers non-traditional versions of hummus to be 'phoney imposters', has published recipes for chickpea spreads that do away with the tahini element and incorporate spices such as cinnamon and ginger. Reluctantly, he states: 'I couldn't help but call them anything other than, well, "hummus".'[1]

Hummus, as a wholesome, nutritious purée, has become a popular food for babies in the West.

The British chef and food writer Nigella Lawson has also created an unorthodox recipe for hummus in which peanut butter replaces tahini, being combined with chickpeas, garlic, lemon juice, cumin and Greek yoghurt. She describes it as being 'elegant' and 'gorgeously filling', coyly asking her reader: 'Is it dreadful to say I prefer this?'[2] Unusual as her recipe may sound, there is a definite flavour logic to Nigella's peanut butter hummus, and the chickpea–peanut formula works well in other contexts. Sudanese falafel, for example, is often served with a rich, savoury peanut sauce that essentially replaces the hummus component of Levantine versions and works perfectly in combination with all the flavours and textures of a falafel sandwich.

It must be noted, however, that this twenty-first-century revolution of hummus flavours has not been felt back home in the Levant, where classic hummus is as popular as it has been for centuries. It has rather been the result of European and American food cultures, a revolution that has taken place in the space of just a couple of decades. As far as these food markets are concerned, the blended combination of chickpeas and tahini is a perfect base to which more flavours – and often dominant flavours – may be added.

At this point it is interesting to compare the medieval recipes for highly spiced and flavoured chickpea and tahini purées with the numerous hummus varieties available in supermarkets today, as well as the abundant recipes for different kinds of hummus listed in modern cookbooks and on the Internet. The addition of coriander, ginger or cinnamon for example, such as we find in today's Moroccan spiced hummus, is considered an innovation – an outrage! – by hummus purists. But Arabic cookbooks from the thirteenth and fourteenth centuries confirm that coriander, ginger and cinnamon were popular flavourings for chickpea and tahini dishes in medieval times. This interplay between the medieval and the modern provides a nice illustration of the ever-changing nature of food culture, which develops under a number of different influences and is not static. New dishes borrow from old ones, which in their turn once borrowed from dishes even older. There was *hummus kasa*, then *hummus bi-tahina*, and now there is hummus – which can be prepared plain or flavoured with spices, herbs or vegetables, creamy or low fat, and even (as we will see below) savoury or sweet.

If coriander, ginger and cinnamon in hummus are cause for outcry among purists, how much more so the indulgent dessert flavours of chocolate and caramel. In recent years hummus has taken yet another direction, being rebranded as a sweet food with the addition of various ingredients (and the obvious omission of garlic). Tahini is naturally compatible with sweet flavours, as anyone who has tried a soft, tahini-stuffed medjool date, tahini cookies or indeed halva will confirm. Chickpeas, being neither inherently sweet nor savoury, can even be eaten as sweets: consider the roasted and sugar-coated chickpeas enjoyed across the Levant and elsewhere in the Middle East. The Lebanese-French chef Karim Haidar of the Paris restaurant Askini has used sweet chickpeas creatively, making a hummus ice cream as well as a milky chickpea dessert similar to rice pudding.[3] Chickpeas have the kind of starchy consistency that allows them to add healthy bulk to sweet foods (in the same way that energy balls can be packed with ground nuts or desiccated coconut, or brownies made with mashed sweet potato). In the age of raw, vegan blondie bites, as well as a kind of reverence for protein, it's not hard to see how chocolate hummus came about.

The American company Delighted By was among the first to make a name for sweet hummus in the snack and dessert market. Delighted By's hummus was first available to

Israeli-style tahini biscuits are just one way of using tahini in combination with sweet flavours.

purchase in three varieties: chocolate, vanilla and snicker-doodle. A number of other American companies followed suit, and several of the major American hummus producers now have a sweet range (including Tribe and Lantana). These days the UK has a sweet hummus offering of its own from the London-based HOU, likewise boasting three flavours, in this case choc-o-chick, banoffee and mixed berry. Choc-o-chick and mixed berry do away with the tahini element altogether, containing chickpeas alongside other ingredients such as cocoa, chocolate, coconut milk, strawberries, blueberries and blue poppyseed. The banoffee flavour, however, retains both chickpeas and tahini, with the additional flavours of banana and caramel. The serving suggestions for these three dips include spreading them on toast for breakfast, eating them with fruit as a tasty snack or consuming straight from the pot as a kind of creamy pudding. Delighted By has even more creative ideas for consuming dessert hummus, from dipping

In recent years several varieties of sweet hummus have appeared in flavours such as chocolate and mixed berry.

frozen hummus balls into melted chocolate to using sweet hummus as a frosting for sugar cookies.

Responses to sweet hummus have been mixed, however, with many finding the chickpea flavour overwhelming or simply not well matched to the other ingredients. Others have found that creating sweet varieties of hummus takes the concept too far, whether or not they taste at all palatable. Writing in the Jewish online magazine *Tablet*, Liel Leibovitz has commented:

> If we want our cross-cultural excursions to mean anything, in the kitchen and beyond, we must acknowledge the existence of boundaries before we cross them. To say 'hey, in my culture we whip up artichoke and spinach with cream, which would kind of go neatly with your mashed chickpea thing' is to approach matters boldly

but respectfully, as two distinct cultures seeking to build bridges should do. To say 'hey, let's make a pudding and call it hummus because hummus is kind of trendy right now' is to exert the tyranny of marketing on a product that has little or no relation to the real thing. It's just in bad taste.[4]

Nonetheless, however unorthodox red pepper or even strawberry hummus may be, they do at least contain the essential ingredient that gives hummus its name: chickpeas. In the age of global love for hummus, however, it appears that hummus in the West often requires no *hummus* at all. As the Western consumer's love for eating the popular dip has grown, so too has the definition of hummus been broadened to include all kinds of tasty combinations of ground vegetables, pulses, spices and herbs. 'Hummus', in this sense, can simply be used to mean 'paste', 'dip' or 'spread'.

Anna Jones's wonderful cookbook *A Modern Way to Eat* (2014) contains a double-page spread on 'hummus', providing four different recipes, none of them containing chickpeas or tahini.[5] One combines cannellini beans, dates and miso, another butter beans, almonds and rosemary. Delicious combinations no doubt, but can we (or should we) call them hummus? In this instance the question concerns language, and while it would be counterintuitive for an Arabic or Hebrew speaker to call a dish of mashed cannellini beans 'hummus', there is no such association for the speakers of other languages.

This new meaning and usage of the term 'hummus' is all part of the new identity the dish has developed in becoming a global food, an industrialized snack, and a multi-flavoured spread and dip. What's more, this usage of the term 'hummus' also illustrates just how popular it has become, and how deeply it has been naturalized to form part of Western food culture in the twenty-first century. When Claudia Roden described a recipe for a dip made from haricot beans, olive oil, lemon juice and black olives in her *Book of Middle Eastern Food* (1968), she called it a 'Purée of Haricot Beans' rather than a haricot bean olive hummus – no doubt because she herself had chickpea-based associations with the word 'hummus' and because 'hummus' was not yet established in the English language as another word for a dip or purée.

To this end, as much as we can claim hummus has become popular in Western food culture, we must likewise acknowledge that it has undergone significant reinvention, which has often stripped it of its component parts and made it into something quite different. Compare, for example, a traditional Neapolitan pizza Margherita – mozzarella, tomatoes, and a tender wheat-flour crust – to a cauliflower-crusted, pumpkin seed-pesto topped 'pizza'. 'Pizza', in this context, is essentially a descriptive term for a food composed of a flat base, sauce and toppings. In much the same way, I recently saw a pan-cooked dish of green vegetables topped with coconut yoghurt and avocado described as a 'vegan shakshuka', despite the lack of tomatoes, peppers, eggs and indeed any ingredient that generally features in a dish by that name. It was described as a 'shakshuka' (I assume) primarily because of the flat cooking pan and inclusion of toppings – and perhaps also because there is no natural descriptive term for a dish of that kind, which is neither traditional to any cuisine nor well established. A 'hummus' today in the context of Western food culture is a smooth dip or paste that can be sweet or savoury, usually based on chickpeas or other pulses, with the addition of vegetables, herbs, spices, fruit or other ingredients. The term is, in essence, simply a more appetizing way of describing a wholesome mush.

In the age of globalization, regional cuisines have spread worldwide. Twenty-first-century city life offers endless varieties of restaurants and eateries from around the globe – not to mention the rapid increase in availability of international products in shops and supermarkets. Ready meals, sauces, condiments and other products are all available at the consumer's convenience. And besides shopping, eating out and ordering at home, unfamiliar recipes can be found online in an instant, offering new possibilities for adventurous home cooking. As regional cuisines have been popularized outside their countries of origin, individual dishes have been adapted (or reinvented) to suit local tastes, incorporating popular flavours and non-traditional ingredients (smoked salmon and cream cheese sushi, I'm looking at you).

Away from the constraints of 'traditional cuisine' there is little emphasis on remaining faithful to the original version of a dish; experimental versions are often popular because they offer the consumer something new to try. In this sense, your local European or American supermarket will sell you

Supermarkets today stock all manner of global foods.

hummus made with sweet potato and coriander – maybe even chocolate hummus – but your local Lebanese restaurant will only offer the traditional, classic *hummus bi-tahina*. This dish will be freshly made, eaten as part of a meze, and served straight up or topped with chickpeas, tahini or grilled meat. In the Levant there is a sense of pride in producing classic hummus to a high standard and no attempt or inclination to invent new flavours. Even Israeli chefs, who enjoy putting a twist on a classic Middle Eastern dish, rarely touch hummus further than to top it with something unusual. If the West has reinvented hummus as a snack food, it has also made it into a vehicle for different flavour combinations, a simple formula to which other ingredients may be added.

In the last few years, however, the Western food market has also seen hummus make its way into main meals, becoming a more substantial player at the dinner table. The rise of bowl food – or Buddha bowls – has put hummus on the map as a healthy vegan and vegetarian food and an excellent part of a balanced plant-based meal. In the context of a mixed bowl, hummus can sit happily alongside rice, quinoa, sweet potato, avocado, raw vegetables, sprouts, beans, seeds or indeed any other wholesome plant-based food. It has perhaps become a major player in a vegan bowl because it not only packs protein, fats and carbohydrates, but goes well with so many foods: everything tastes good with hummus. These kinds of eating habits – in combination with the culture of dips and snacking – are by and large the domain of the younger generations. Indeed, even supermarket sales of hummus in the UK have been shown to be significantly lower among those aged over 44.[6]

Hummus is undoubtedly a food for our times. In response to the climate crisis and inhumane treatment of factory-farmed animals many conscientious eaters have cut out or massively reduced their consumption of meat, dairy, fish and eggs. Others have adopted plant-based diets for reasons related to health. Pulses, including chickpeas, beans and lentils, are an extremely important source of protein for those eating little to no animals products. What's more, they are a highly sustainable option (as are sesame seeds). Eating hummus, therefore, is good for body, planet and animal welfare.

Indeed, even growing the chickpeas needed for hummus can be beneficial to farmers' overall production rates: the cultivation of chickpeas enriches the soil with nitrogen, acting like a fertilizer and helping other crops to thrive. Rotating the cultivation of maize and other cereals with that of chickpeas and other legumes has been shown to produce a better yield of the former. This is because nodules on the roots of the legume plants are home to bacteria that transform nitrogen in the air into a form in the soil that facilitates plant growth. Different legume and cereal crops can also be planted in rows or intermixed, producing similar results in the quality of the soil. Whichever technique is used, cultivating chickpeas has the potential to improve the yields of other crops and is far more practical and profitable than employing expensive fertilizers for the same purpose.

Hummus – as a snack, a meal, a sandwich filling, part of a meze or a component of a Buddha bowl – is a wholesome,

The cultivation of chickpeas is beneficial to that of other crops: the chickpea plants convert nitrogen in the air into a plant-accessible form in the soil.

filling and inexpensive plant-based option. It is easy to prepare at home and requires very few ingredients. Purists can eat it as it is, with a good swirl of olive oil and a warm pitta, and those who like it flavoured can add beetroot, turmeric or any other ingredient: your hummus, your choice.

Recipes

The recipes below each call for around 500 grams (3 cups) of cooked chickpeas. To achieve this with dried chickpeas, you must start the night before, soaking 225 grams (1¼ cups) of chickpeas in a large bowl of water. The next day drain and rinse the chickpeas, before adding them to a large cooking pan with ½ tsp bicarbonate of soda and stirring on a high heat until you've heard them sizzle for a couple of minutes. Next add 1 litre (4¼ cups) of fresh water to the pan, covering the chickpeas generously, and bring to the boil before finally reducing the heat to a simmer. The chickpeas will take some 30 minutes to become soft enough for hummus, though the cooking time can vary and it is best to check them fairly often. When the chickpeas are thoroughly softened, drain them, reserving their cooking water for later. You'll find that a large proportion of the chickpea skins come loose during cooking and can be easily removed (whether or not to tackle the others is your own decision – personally, I don't).

Alternatively, if time is short or dried chickpeas are missing from your store cupboard or pantry, two tins or jars of chickpeas will do fine. Empty the contents (including the water) into a pan, add a splash of fresh water and simmer for around ten minutes on a low heat until perfectly soft. Drain, reserving the chickpea water. It is worth bearing in mind that some tins or jars of chickpeas contain salt – if using this kind it is best to reduce or omit the salt added in the recipes.

For the recipes that call for tahini, I recommend using a light one (it will be more liquid and have a milder flavour). If in doubt, look for a Lebanese product. It is a good idea to store unopened containers of tahini upside down, because the thick sesame paste has a tendency to separate from the oil (it needs a good stir before being using). If you do get left with a very thick and solid tahini paste at the bottom of the container you can use it to make an instant halva – simply combine the thick tahini with date syrup (or another sweetener) and a pinch of ground vanilla, then mix well, flatten out and store in the fridge.

The quantities used throughout will produce around 3–4 medium-sized bowls of hummus, whether they are served as individual portions for a main meal or as additions to a larger selection of meze. All the recipes can easily be halved to produce a small portion, or increased as much as is required.

The quantities of ingredients are intended only as guidelines and need not be followed exactly – hummus is all about personal preferences and both tasting as you go and adjusting the flavours are heartily encouraged.

Hummus Kasa

The first two recipes are based on the medieval ones given in the first chapter, though I have added measurements according to my own interpretation and omitted the more obscure ingredients, such as rose hips and chopped rue. Preserved lemons should be available in delis and other specialist food shops. Feel free to vary the proportions of one spice or seasoning according to your own taste.

500 g (3 cups) cooked chickpeas
100 g (1 cup) walnuts
1 tsp coriander seed
1 tsp caraway seed
4 tbsp tahini
4 tbsp wine vinegar
3 tbsp lemon juice
1 small bunch parsley

1 small bunch mint
1 tbsp olive oil
1 tsp cinnamon
1 tsp ground pepper
1 tsp ginger
2 preserved lemons
50 g (½ cup) pistachios

Setting aside a few whole chickpeas, crush the remainder with a ladle or purée them in the food processor before adding to a large mixing bowl. Gently toast the walnuts in a pan along with the coriander and caraway seeds. Once toasted, pound the walnuts and seeds in a pestle and mortar (or grind in a food processor) and add to the mixing bowl. Then add the tahini, vinegar and lemon juice and mix well.

Next, finely chop the fresh herbs, reserving a little parsley, and add them to the chickpea mixture, stirring in the olive oil and remaining spices as you do so. Finely mince the preserved lemons and add these to the bowl, stirring well. The mixture will be considerably thicker than *hummus bi-tahina*. To serve, set the whole mixture out onto a plate like a pâté and liberally season with olive oil. Chop the pistachios and sprinkle these over the chickpea mixture. Take the reserved whole chickpeas and chopped parsley and sprinkle these over, too. If you like, you can also dust with a little ground cinnamon. Serve spread thickly onto crusty bread.

Thirteenth-century Chickpeas with Ginger and Cinnamon

Unlike *hummus kasa*, there is no tahini in this medieval recipe. However, like the *hummus bi-tahina* we eat today, the chickpeas are puréed into a kind of smooth dip that can be eaten with bread and other foods.

500 g (3 cups) cooked chickpeas
2 tbsp wine vinegar

2 tsp cinnamon
2 tsp ground pepper
2 tsp ground ginger
4 pickled lemons
1 small bunch parsley
1 small bunch mint
olive oil (to garnish)

Purée the chickpeas in a food processor or blender incorporating a little of the cooking water and tip the puree into a fairly large serving bowl. Stir in the vinegar and spices and enough extra cooking water to produce a smooth and creamy result. Carefully slice the skins off the pickled lemons and chop the pulp, adding this to the chickpea mixture. Next finely chop the fresh herbs and add these too. Finally, spread the purée out across the sides of the bowl with the back of a spoon and generously season with olive oil. Serve with warm bread for dipping.

Classic Hummus with Tahini and Chickpeas

For this recipe I've used Claudia Rodin and Yotam Ottolenghi's versions as a guide – but really, making simple hummus is all about tasting, checking the flavours and adjusting to your liking. Personally, I like hummus very smooth and creamy, with plenty of tahini and lemon and a little less garlic. But feel free to play around with the exact proportions and find your own perfect hummus. The best way to do this is to add the ingredients little by little (for example, start with one lemon and one small clove of garlic) and continue tasting until it's just how you like it.

500 g (3 cups) cooked chickpeas
200 g (1 cup) tahini (plus 2 tbsp)
1–2 lemons
1–2 cloves garlic
salt

paprika
a little parsley
olive oil

Start by setting aside a few chickpeas to scatter over the final dish. Then take 2 tbsp of tahini and mix well in a small bowl with a splash of fresh water and a squeeze of lemon juice. The tahini will split and then become pale coloured and creamy: it should be liquid enough to drizzle. Setting the tahini bowl aside, add the remaining chickpeas to the blender, along with the juice of 1 lemon, 1 clove of garlic, a pinch of salt and a little of the chickpea cooking water. Blend until smooth and then add the larger quantity of tahini and another splash of the cooking water. Blend again until everything is combined. Taste and check the consistency – it should be thick but still creamy. If you like, you can add more garlic, lemon, salt or cooking water at this point and blend again until everything is smooth. To serve, spread the room-temperature hummus around the base and sides of individual bowls, leaving a hollow in the middle. Season liberally with olive oil, scatter the chickpeas, drizzle the thinned lemon tahini and sprinkle with paprika and chopped parsley. Eat with warmed pitta or other flatbreads and a selection of fresh and pickled vegetables.

Alternatively, to make your bowl of hummus into a more filling meal, you can also top it with a quartered hard-boiled egg in addition to the chickpeas and tahini. For a simple and delicious variation, add a small bunch of parsley (leaves finely chopped) to the hummus during the blending stage. For a sweeter-tasting hummus, Nada Saleh even suggests replacing the lemons with squeezed oranges or clementines – she recommends the use of Seville oranges for a particularly exceptional flavour. And to add a little crunch and freshness to your meal of hummus, you can't go wrong with a simple Levantine salad of chopped tomato, cucumber, pepper and radish dressed with olive oil, lemon juice and a pinch of salt.

Musabbaha/mashawsha

A kind of deconstructed hummus, this dish is extremely popular
in the Levant and easy to prepare at home to be eaten at any time
of day. The chickpeas simply need to be a little firmer than they
do for making hummus, because most of them are served whole
here, with only a handful being puréed. The dish is served warm,
with a lemony tahini sauce.

500 g (3 cups) cooked chickpeas
150 g (¾ cup) tahini
1 lemon
1 clove garlic
1 tsp cumin
salt
a little parsley
paprika
olive oil

Begin by removing 125 g (¾ cup) of cooked chickpeas to make
a small portion of hummus, setting the rest aside for later. Blend
the smaller quantity of chickpeas along with 50 g (¼ cup) tahini, the
juice of ½ lemon, ½ clove of garlic, cumin, a pinch of salt and a
splash of cooking water. Check the taste and consistency and then
set the hummus aside. Next mix the remaining 100 g of tahini with
the juice of ½ lemon, ½ crushed clove of garlic and enough fresh
water to make a smooth, creamy (and relatively liquid) tahini sauce.
If the whole chickpeas and hummus have cooled down by the time
you want to eat them, warm them up a little before serving. Spoon
some warm hummus into each dish or bowl, add a generous portion of whole chickpeas and drizzle with the tahini sauce until
covered. Finally, season with olive oil and add a good scattering of
chopped parsley and a sprinkle of paprika. Serve with pitta or
other bread suitable for scooping.

Butternut Squash and Nigella Seed Hummus

I rarely make flavoured hummus at home, but the sweet, earthy notes of squash are particularly good in combination with chickpeas (and tahini). The nigella seeds are a surprise note here, and also look especially striking sprinkled over the pale orange-coloured hummus. If butternut squash are unavailable you could use roasted pumpkin, carrots or even sweet potato here.

1 butternut squash
500 g (3 cups) cooked chickpeas
1–2 cloves garlic
1–2 lemons
2 tsp nigella seeds
salt
200 g (1 cup) tahini
olive oil
a little parsley

Start by preparing the butternut squash – wash the skin well, slice (removing the seeds in the middle) and place the slices on a baking tray. Drizzle with olive oil and roast in the oven at around 190°C (375°F) until soft and lightly browned at the edges (this should take between twenty minutes and half an hour). You will need 200 g (1 cup) of roasted squash to blend into the hummus, plus a few extra slices to put on top. The rest of the squash may be used for another dish.

Reserving a few chickpeas for the topping, add the rest to the blender, along with the juice of 1 lemon, 1 clove of garlic, 200 g (1 cup) roasted butternut squash, 1 tsp nigella seeds, a pinch of salt and a little of the chickpea water. Blend until combined and smooth. Then add the tahini and another splash of water and blend again. Check the flavours and consistency and adjust as desired. Serve in the traditional way, smoothed out around the edges of a bowl and topped with a drizzle of olive oil. Add a scattering of whole chickpeas, a few small slices of roast squash, a sprinkling of parsley and a few extra nigella seeds.

Maple Vanilla Hummus

Following the trend for 'dessert hummus', I've included my own recipe for a sweet variation here, using maple syrup, vanilla, cashew butter and lemon zest. The resulting flavour and texture is similar to that of a vegan cheesecake: this hummus is best enjoyed spread generously over a plain sweet biscuit and topped with a few raspberries.

500 g (3 cups) cooked chickpeas
75 ml (¼ cup) maple syrup
½ tsp ground vanilla
juice of 1 lemon and zest of ½ lemon
150 g (¾ cup) tahini
50 g (¼ cup) cashew butter

Add the chickpeas to the blender, along with the maple syrup, vanilla, lemon juice and zest and a splash of freshwater. Blend until smooth and then add the tahini and cashew butter. Blend again, incorporating a little more water if the mixture is too thick. Allow the hummus to set in the fridge before serving.

Aquafaba: A Hummus By-product

The water in which chickpeas are cooked (or the water from a chickpea tin or jar) is known as aquafaba (from the Latin *aqua* (water) and *faba* (beans)), an ingredient in its own right. The water from other tins of cooked pulses may also be used as aquafaba, though that of chickpeas appears to yield the most successful results as a culinary ingredient. The hummus recipes above use aquafaba to thin the blended combination of chickpeas and tahini, but this enriched cooking water can be put to many other uses thanks to its high carbohydrate and protein content. In recent years aquafaba has become a popular egg-white replacement in vegan and egg-free cooking. It can be used in place of egg for meringues, macarons, mousse, marshmallows, mayonnaise and many other things, including waffles, ice cream, brownies and cookies. Food blogs and vegan cookbooks alike are awash with aquafaba recipes – it shouldn't be hard to find one you like. The best part, of course, is that aquafaba makes a great addition to a waste-free or low-waste kitchen, being an ingredient that is otherwise discarded.

References

1 When Chickpeas Met Tahini

1 Christopher Cumo, *Foods That Changed History: How Foods Shaped Civilization from the Ancient World to the Present* (Santa Barbara, CA, and Denver, CO, 2015), p. 70.
2 Charles Perry has shared this theory with me in personal correspondence.
3 Charles Perry, *Scents and Flavors: A Syrian Cookbook* (New York, 2017), pp. 129–30.
4 Charles Perry, 'The Description of Familiar Foods', in Maxime Rodinson, A. J. Arberry and Charles Perry, *Medieval Arab Cookery* (Devon, 2001), p. 383.
5 Lilia Zaouali, *Medieval Cuisine of the Islamic World* (Berkeley, CA, 2007), p. 65.
6 See Diana Spechler, 'Who Invented Hummus?', www.bbc.com (12 December 2017).

2 Hummus at Home

1 Mohammad Orfali, 'Hummus Has Its Memories', in Ariel Rosenthal, Orly Peli-Bronshtein and Dan Alexander, *On the Hummus Route* (n.p., 2019), p. 385.
2 Anissa Helou, 'Hommus Khawali', www.anissas.com, accessed 18 August 2011.

3 Farouk Mardam-Bey, 'The Only Important Question
   to Ask', in Rosenthal et al., *On the Hummus Route*, p. 383.
4 Helou, 'Hommus Khawali'.
5 Deb Perelman, 'Ethereally Smooth Hummus',
   www.smittenkitchen.com, 8 January 2013.
6 Nof Atamna-Ismaeel, 'The Joy of Growing Chickpeas',
   in Rosenthal et al., *On the Hummus Route*, p. 271.
7 Orfali, 'Hummus Has Its Memories', p. 386.
8 Nada Saleh, *New Flavours of the Lebanese Table* (London,
   2007), p. x.
9 Mousa Tawfiq, 'A Poor Man's Kebab', in Rosenthal et al.,
   On the Hummus Route, p. 77.

3 Spreading the Hummus

1 Katy Salter, 'The British Love Affair with Hummus',
   www.theguardian.com, 7 August 2013.
2 Tom De Castella, 'How Hummus Conquered Britain',
   www.bbc.com, 7 October 2011.
3 Elizabeth David, *A Book of Mediterranean Food* (London,
   1950), pp. 152–3.
4 Claudia Roden, *A Book of Middle Eastern Food* (London,
   1968), pp. 83–4.
5 Claudia Roden, 'London's Mongrel English Cuisine',
   AA Files, 49 (Spring 2003), p. 68.
6 Joan Nathan and Judy Stacey Goldman, *The Flavor of
   Jerusalem* (Boston, MA, and Toronto, 1974), p. 46.
7 'Happy Birthday Houmous!', www.waitrose.com,
   25 April 2018.
8 Felicity Cloake, 'Dip Back In: Beat the Hummus Crisis
   with this Quick Recipe', www.theguardian.com,
   26 April 2017.
9 De Castella, 'How Hummus Conquered Britain'.
10 Justin R. Silverman, 'Hummus's Quest to Conquer
   America, One Mouth at a Time', www.today.com,
   20 April 2016.

11 Scott Goodson, 'The Surprising Rise of Hummus in America', www.huffpost.com, 5 June 2015.

12 Deb Perelman, 'Hummus Heaped with Tomatoes and Cucumbers', www.smittenkitchen.com, 18 July 2017.

13 Silverman, 'Hummus's Quest to Conquer America, One Mouth at a Time'.

4 War and Peas

1 Ari Ariel, 'The Hummus Wars', *Gastronomica*, XXII/1 (Spring 2012), p. 37.

2 See Ronald Ranta and Yonatan Mendel, 'Consuming Palestine: Palestine and Palestinians in Israeli Food Culture', *Ethnicities*, XIV/3 (June 2014), p. 422.

3 Quoted in Ariel, 'The Hummus Wars', p. 34.

4 Quoted ibid., p. 41.

5 Quoted ibid., p. 38.

6 Quoted ibid.

7 Ibid., p. 39.

8 Yotam Ottolenghi and Sami Tamimi, *Jerusalem* (London, 2012), p. 16.

9 Ibid.

10 Diala Shaheen, 'About', www.thehummustheory.com.

11 Ariel Rosenthal, 'Hummus and Me – It's Personal', in Ariel Rosenthal, Orly Peli-Bronshtein and Dan Alexander, *On the Hummus Route* (n.p., 2019), p. 168.

12 Ibid., p. 169.

13 Quoted in Ariel, 'The Hummus Wars', p. 36.

5 Generation Hummus

1 Yotam Ottolenghi, 'Yotam Ottolenghi's Hummus Recipes', www.theguardian.com, 7 July 2018.

2 Nigella Lawson, *Nigella Kitchen: Recipes from the Heart of the Home* (London, 2010).

3 Karim Haidar, 'Hummus Without Borders', in Ariel
  Rosenthal, Orly Peli-Bronshtein and Dan Alexander,
  On the Hummus Route (n. p., 2019), p. 351.
4 Liel Leibovitz, 'Chocolate Hummus? Have You No
  Shame?', www.tabletmag.com, 21 February 2018.
5 Anna Jones, *A Modern Way to Eat* (London, 2014),
  pp. 62–3.
6 Tom De Castella, 'How Hummus Conquered Britain',
  www.bbc.com, 7 October 2011.

Bibliography

Ariel, Ari, 'The Hummus Wars', *Gastronomica*, xii/1
    (Spring 2012), pp. 34–42

Cloake, Felicity, 'Dip Back In: Beat the Hummus Crisis with this
    Quick Recipe', www.theguardian.com (26 April 2017)

Cumo, Christopher, *Foods That Changed History: How Foods Shaped
    Civilization from the Ancient World to the Present* (Santa Barbara,
    CA, and Denver, CO, 2015)

David, Elizabeth, *A Book of Mediterranean Food* (London, 1950)

De Castella, Tom, 'How Hummus Conquered Britain', www.bbc.
    com, 7 October 2011

Goodson, Scott, 'The Surprising Rise of Hummus in America',
    www.huffpost.com, 5 June 2015

'Happy Birthday Houmous!', www.waitrose.com, 25 April 2018

Helou, Anissa, www.anissas.com

Hirsch, Dafna, '"Hummus Is Best When It's Fresh and Made
    by Arabs": The Gourmetization of Hummus in Israel and
    the Return of the Repressed Arab', *American Ethnologist*,
    xxxviii/4 (November 2011), pp. 617–30

'Hummus Market 2020: Top Countries Data, Global Analysis,
    Market Size, Growth, Definition, Opportunities and
    Forecast to 2024', www.marketwatch.com, 28 February 2020

Jones, Anna, *A Modern Way to Eat* (London, 2014)

Lawson, Nigella, *Nigella Kitchen: Recipes from the Heart of the Home*
    (London, 2010)

Leibovitz, Liel, 'Chocolate Hummus? Have You No Shame?',
    www.tabletmag.com, 21 February 2018

Nathan, Joan, and Judy Stacey Goldman, *The Flavor of Jerusalem*
    (Boston, MA, and Toronto, 1974).
Ottolenghi, Yotam, 'Jerusalem on a Plate: Identity, Tradition,
    and Ownership', *Gastronomica*, XV/1 (Spring 2015),
    pp. 1–7
—, 'Yotam Ottolenghi's Hummus Recipes', www.theguardian.
    com (7 July 2018)
—, and Sami Tamimi, *Jerusalem* (London, 2012)
Perelman, Deb, www.smittenkitchen.com
Perry, Charles, *Scents and Flavors: A Syrian Cookbook*
    (New York, 2017)
Ranta, Ronald, and Yonatan Mendel, 'Consuming Palestine:
    Palestine and Palestinians in Israeli Food Culture', *Ethnicities*,
    XIV/3 (June 2014), pp. 412–35
Roden, Claudia, *The Book of Jewish Food* (New York, 1996)
—, *A Book of Middle Eastern Food* (London, 1968)
—, 'London's Mongrel English Cuisine', *AA Files*, 49 (Spring
    2003), pp. 68–9
Rodinson, Maxime, A. J. Arberry and Charles Perry, *Medieval
    Arab Cookery* (Devon, 2001)
Rosenthal, Ariel, Orly Peli-Bronshtein and Dan Alexander,
    On the Hummus Route (n.p., 2019)
Rossant, Colette, *Apricots on the Nile: A Memoir with Recipes*
    (New York, 1999)
Saleh, Nada, *New Flavours of the Lebanese Table* (London, 2007)
Salter, Katy, 'The British Love Affair with Hummus',
    www.theguardian.com, 7 August 2013
Silverman, Justin R., 'Hummus's Quest to Conquer America,
    One Mouth at a Time', www.today.com, 20 April 2016
Shaheen, Diala, www.thehummustheory.com
Smithers, Rebecca, 'Hummus "Crisis" Sheds Light on Secret
    World of Mass Food Production', www.theguardian.com,
    29 April 2017
Spechler, Diana, 'Who Invented Hummus?', www.bbc.com
    (12 December 2017)
The Story of Food: An Illustrated History of Everything We Eat
    (London, 2018)

Takemura, Alison F., 'How Chickpeas Can Fix Soil and
    Feed Farmers', www.nationalgeographic.com, 8 April 2016
Visser, Margaret, *Much Depends on Dinner* (Toronto, 1986)
Zaouali, Lilia, *Medieval Cuisine of the Islamic World*
    (Berkeley, CA, 2007)

Websites and Associations

Chickpeas and Other Legumes

Pulses
https://pulses.org/global

Pulse Australia
www.pulseaus.com.au

Chickpea Agriculture Today

AgriFutures
www.agrifutures.com.au/farm-diversity/chickpea

USA Pulses
www.usapulses.org

Indian Society of Pulses Research and Development
www.isprd.in/index.html

International Crops Research, Institute for the Semi-arid Tropics
http://exploreit.icrisat.org/profile/Chickpea/232

Global Hummus Enthusiasm

The Hummus Blog
https://humus101.com/EN

For the Love of Hummus
https://fortheloveofhummus.com

Hummus Day
https://hummusday.com

Hummus Memes
https://hummusmemes.com

Acknowledgements

First off, I am immensely grateful to Michael Leaman, Andrew Smith, Amy Salter and all the team at Reaktion Books for making this hummus book possible. I also extend particular thanks to Charles Perry, who has been extremely kind and generous in offering his expertise, especially as concerns the field of medieval Arabic cookbooks and the origins of *hummus bi-tahina* as we know it today. I am grateful to Claudia Roden, whose collective writings have been inspiration for my own studies and research for many years – her ability to combine scholarly food history with personal culinary memories and practical recipe-writing is unparalleled.

I also extend my thanks to my parents, Ralph and Rosemary Publicover, and to my friend Robert Sieben-Tait, all of whom read drafts of this book and returned them to me with many helpful thoughts and comments. Thanks also go to Num Stibbe and Ornan Rotem for their generous provision of both ceramics for food styling and guidance in editing my manuscript. I am grateful to my daughters, Ira and Amalia, for somehow allowing me to find the time to write a book, and for eating a lot of hummus in the name of research. And finally, the biggest thanks go to my partner, Lian, who supported this project from its very conception and encouraged me to write this book. He has helped me at every stage along the way, from setting out the structure to refining the content, as well as providing beautiful original images to accompany the text. I couldn't have thought of a better project to work on with him – though he mostly lets me have free rein in the kitchen, hummus is something we always make together.

Photo Acknowledgements

The author and publishers wish to express their thanks to the below sources of illustrative material and/or permission to reproduce it. Some locations of artworks are also given below, in the interest of brevity:

Photo Anwar Amro/AFP via Getty Images: p. 64; Biblioteca Estense, Modena/World Digital Library (WDL): p. 20; Bibliothèque nationale de France, Paris (Supplément Persan 1113): p. 29; Everett Collection Inc/Alamy Stock Photo: p. 62; Hellenic Institute for Byzantine and Post-Byzantine Studies, Venice (Ven. Inst. Gr. 5, fol. 91r): p. 16; photo levarTravel/Unsplash: p. 74; The Metropolitan Museum of Art, New York: pp. 24, 30; Nationaal Archief, The Hague: p. 53; The National Photo Collection, Government Press Office Photography Department, Jerusalem: p. 67; The New York Public Library: p. 15; photos Harriet Nussbaum: pp. 10, 11, 19, 40, 41, 50, 56, 69, 76, 80, 83, 84, 87; Österreichische Nationalbibliothek, Vienna: p. 17; private collection: p. 31; photos Shutterstock.com: pp. 6 (Anna_Pustynnikova), 14 (Peter Hermes Furian, *top*), 14 (oksana2010, *foot*), 18 (Tukaram.Karve), 22 (Neshama Roash), 27 (vetre), 37 (ozMedia), 38 (cihanyuce), 39 (Bhagith), 42 (MikeDotta), 43 (Barnuti Daniel Ioan), 78 (Liliya Kandrashevich), 89 (Havryliuk-Kharzhevska); photo Juj Winn/Getty Images: p. 35.

Hassan Moussawi (Beyrouthhh), the copyright holder of the image on p. 32, has published it online under conditions imposed by a Creative Commons Attribution 3.0 Unported License. Eitan

Index

italic numbers refer to illustrations; **bold** to recipes